Book 4:
Soccer Coaching Knowledge

Academy of Coaching Soccer Skills and Fitness Drills

Bert Holcroft

Order this book online at www.trafford.com
or email orders@trafford.com

Most Trafford titles are also available at major online book retailers.

© Copyright 2019 Bert Holcroft.

All rights reserved. No part of this publication may be reproduced, stored in a retrieval system, or transmitted, in any form or by any means, electronic, mechanical, photocopying, recording, or otherwise, without the written prior permission of the author.

Print information available on the last page.

ISBN: 978-1-4907-8608-7 (sc)

ISBN: 978-1-4907-8607-0 (e)

Because of the dynamic nature of the Internet, any web addresses or links contained in this book may have changed since publication and may no longer be valid. The views expressed in this work are solely those of the author and do not necessarily reflect the views of the publisher, and the publisher hereby disclaims any responsibility for them.

Our mission is to efficiently provide the world's finest, most comprehensive book publishing service, enabling every author to experience success. To find out how to publish your book, your way, and have it available worldwide, visit us online at www.trafford.com

Any people depicted in stock imagery provided by Getty Images are models, and such images are being used for illustrative purposes only.
Certain stock imagery © Getty Images.

Trafford rev. 05/10/2019

 www.trafford.com

North America & international
toll-free: 1 888 232 4444 (USA & Canada)
fax: 812 355 4082

SPORTS REVELATIONS ENTERPRISES -
Rugby Accreditation
Learn@Home Project

Bert Holcroft
Course Co-ordinator

Academy of Excellence
Foreword by Sir Clive Woodward OBE
WORLD ACCREDITED COACHING SEMINAR
www.sportsrevent.com

Bert & Margo Holcroft - Authors   Copyright © 2012 Sports Revelations Enterprises

SCIENTIFIC - ANALYSIS

SO YOU WANT TO BE AN INTERNATIONAL RUGBY OR SOCCER PLAYER?

Rugby Accreditation

SCIENTIFIC & FITNESS RUGBY REVELATIONS
PERSONAL TRAINER-FITNESS FOR SOCCER

1	FUTURISTIC "FIFTEEN MAN RUGBY"
2	ADVANCED FUTURISTIC "RUGBY-LEAGUE"
3	FUTURISTIC FITNESS REVELATIONS
4	PERSONAL TRAINER SOCCER-FITNESS REVELATIONS

"RUGBY REVEL ATIONS"
VIRTUAL REALITY IN CYBER SPACE
ARTISTIC EXPRESSIONS OF FUTURISTIC
INNOVATIVE TECHNICAL PROFICIENCIES
ILLUSTRATED DEPICTING ELITE
FINESSE FOR "SPORTS EXCELLENCE"
By ACCREDITED GRADE III COACH—BERT HOLCROFT.

E-mail: bert@sportsrevent.com
Web sites: www.sportsrevent.com
www.futuristicrugby.com
Authors and Publishers: BERT & MARGO HOLCROFT © Copyright 2007.
Pre-print Preparation and Additional Design: COLLINS & DARWELL LTD.
Telephone 01942 673166 • E-mail: info@collinsanddarwell.co.uk
Website Design and Hosting: www.tylmail.com
Manual Images: Nathan Kilburn—Email: mr.claypole@ntlworld.com
Print and Design: ROBERTS ARTWORK
Telephone 0161-281 6468 • E-mail: robertsartwork@btinternet.com

FUTURISTIC-SOCCER & FITNESS REVELATIONS
FOREWORD BY JIMMY SMITH

Ex Burnley, Fulham & Leyton Orient, Professional Soccer Player AccreditedF.A Coaching Certificates also Ex Ranked R.A.F Physical-Training Instructor, i.e. P.T.I.

My Personal Experience and Accreditations

I have been involved in Association Football at every level of playing, coaching & Administration—Amateur and Professional—for 40 years.

I signed on as a junior apprentice for Burnley F.C., I have had the good fortune to Play with and against many famous players in mycareer, the likes of Sir Stanley Matthews, Tommy Lawton, etc., etc. My family and I have been involved in promoting soccer for more than 100 years. That is my grandad, my father Jimmy Smith & myself, you could call us football centurions.

I have assisted Bert Holcroft in the formation of this unique book on Soccer and Fitness for Soccer,as a consultant and adviser on the technical proficiencies, skills and drills featured in the excellent text, depicting illustrations of futuristic impressions of soccer.

This book is, in my opinion, unsurpassed with its mountain of information & technology.

Any interested person intent on improving his soccer skills and fitness levels should purchase this invaluable source of information—that is if one is ambitious enough to aim at professionalism or even to improve one's participation in a game of soccer at any level.

I am happy to recommend this book and its content.

Revelations the like of which have previously been reserved only for the privileged few i.e. the top professional stars, who's well-paid coaches, exercise physiologists, psychologists & nutritionists are at these players' "beck and call".

This book now reveals these Clinical Professional Secrets to you, the public.

Good Luck in your sporting endeavour.

PRE-Soccer—Fitness—Revelations

INTRODUCTION—"PERSONALFITNESSTRAINER" FORSOCCER TRANSFORMATION IN THE NEW MILLENIUM

In past years, pre-war and early post-war, the accepted formula for "Tactics and Strategies in Soccer", were formulated around the tactical (5x3x2) plan.

The changes came with the introduction of the "European game to Britain", the "Europeans" and the "Continentals", introduced new positional formats, Completely different tactical field positions, than the previous accepted (5x3x2) game plan. The new formats and positional changes were adopted by the "British Coaches" as the "Holy Grail of Futuristic Soccer". These changing formats revolutionized the whole concept of previous positional play, and placed greater demand on the players "fitness levels"!

These new modern formations also placed great emphasis on player movements, they introduced mobility and flexibility amongst their players by asking them to participate in "Defence and Attack". European and Continental Coaches created these innovative strategies and integrating positional changes by using attacking players to assist in defence, and defensive players to assist in attacking moves. This concept of multiple positional changes during a game, transformed the British game by demanding from its players a greater all around fitness and involvement in both "Attack and Defence". Managers, Coaches and Conditioners realised that player's fitness levels had to be changed dramatically, the Professional Clubs all of a sudden had to employ a clinical level of expertise, in came "Exercise Physiologist"—"Sports Psychologists", "Sports Therapists"—"Nutritionists" and additional training aids, such as "progressive resistance exercises", (using previous taboo of "Weight-Training) i.e. sprint resistance sleds, back-packs, innovating a complete new format of ("Aerobic") and ("An-Aerobic") exercises, ("plyodynamics"), ("plyokinetics"), ("sprint-training"), (endurance training), (agility), (flexibility), (strength) and "power-drills", all of a sudden these modern fitness innovations became the norm, inevitably these new additions had to be implemented to increase the capacity of their player's fitness levels to cope with this new format of "Soccer Revelations".

Players own personal realisations suddenly took a complete change towards fitness assessments, as Coaches and Managers realised that players were expected to run further and faster during every game, (instead of their previous minimal involvement),they had to change their appraisals and promote a complete reversal of their previous training i.e.times, days, energy systems and equipment.

These new formats demanded more physical involvement to implement, placing a greater exertion on "Energy Systems", and on the players "Body Systems". It soon became quite evident that a whole new fitness regime had materialised. It became obvious, to maintain your position in a team would mean accepting these new fitness levels and changes. The word "Exercise Physiology", would have to be accepted, and promoted, higher percentages of the "Nine Levels of Fitness", would have to become a priority. Every player would now have to be aware that, higher levels of "Fitness and Endurance", as well as "Technical Proficiencies", would be a "pre-requisite", to become involved in this modernistic football. May I predict that in the future professional soccer players will be elevated into the realms of fantasy, all "star players", who have achieved this status, would demand "Mega Bucks" for their services. With the intervention of the European "Bill of Rights", relating to employment ethics and "F.I.F.A.'s" rulings on the proposed transfer system, these star players will be surrounded by a consortium of personal consultants such as (Managers) (Lawyers), (Accountants), (P.R. persons) i.e. (T/V etc), (Business Consultants), along with the player's own personal training consortium i.e. "Exercise Physiologists", "Sports Psychologists", "Sports Therapists" and "Nutritionists",(all at academic levels of learning). The player's most important addition, would be his "Personal Fitness Trainer", it would be up to this person to make sure his charges (attain), (maintain) and (sustain), a very high level of "superior fitness", so that they can maintain their status as "Super Stars", these "Super Stars" will also have another source of information. These additional experts are; "Video Analysts" and "Technical Proficiency Advisors", employed specifically to monitor their game with the implementations of complex innovative additions to football, changing the whole scenario. Professional clubs, with the (24year old) (FIFIA Rule) i.e. (for retaining contracted players), will target (schoolboy—football) and junior players as young as (13 years of age) will be recruited by scouts. Pro footballers—valid expectancy, in their new professional era, will be a short (15 years) up to the age of (28)! All futuristic Team Managers will aim for an average age limit of (22 years) promoting (28 years old) available only for the very experienced categories, maybe (one or two positions) in a defensive roll could be filled by these senior footballers. With this evolution in mind I have written this "Personal Fitness and Technical Proficiency Football Manual", so that every person interested in football can achieve, "Mega Stardom Status" and "Elite Fitness For Futuristic Soccer".

This book is the "pre-requisite and key", toopen the door of future players "Mega Bucks Earnings Capacity". The cascade of defined informative and illustrated chapters, introduces, "(Physiology")", (Psychology), (Technology), i.e. (Skills), (Nutrition), (Progressive Resistance Training) etc, giving the interested person, the opportunity to achieve previously unattainable goals.

(Sport and Fitness Guru)—Bert Holcroft.

EFFECTIVE ADMINISTRATION.

PROFESSIONAL SPORTING ORGANISATIONS.
Compiled by Bert Holcroft.

The leader of an organisation, particularly the chairman, must be concerned about two important functions within a meeting. They are:

Task: **Getting good decisions made from which action will follow.**

Relationships: **Ensuring that members are happy with the meeting and each other. They have been heard and accept the decision made.**

There is an appropriate degree of FORMALITY for a meeting. Factors suggesting a more formal meeting are large number of people, limited time, diversity of views, importance of matter being discussed, members are strangers to each other.

SUCCESSFUL SPORTING ADMINISTRATION.

1. Objects of the Sporting Organisation.
2. Roles of the Key Office Bearers.
3. Accounting Systems Treasurer.
4. Financial Planning.
5. Budgeting.
6. Cash Flow.
7. Financial Control.
8. Forward Planning.
9. Statutory Obligations.

SPORTING ORGANISATIONS.

1. OBJECTS OF A SPORTING ORGANISATION.

The Memorandum and Articles of Association, Rules and By-Laws or the Constitution will clearly state the objectives of the sporting organisation. Of course, the objectives of the different organisations will vary greatly, however as sporting administrators, you each must be fully acquainted with the objects of your particular organisation and work within the boundaries of those objectives in order to achieve desired goals.

OBJECTS

The Objects of the Soccer/Football Club should be:

To promote the game of soccer/football and to secure, make and maintain provision to enable members and their sons to play **soccer/football**.

To secure, provide and maintain a club for the use and enjoyment of members and their guests.

To provide accommodation, conveniences and amenities as well as food and refreshments for members and their guests and

To promote and provide entertainment and facilities for such social and literary activities and such other sporting and athletic pastimes as may be decided upon by the General Committee or by the Members in general meeting.

2. ROLES OF THE KEY OFFICE BEARERS.

Office Bearers are usually elected by the members attending a properly constituted annual general meeting of the particular organisation. In most cases, the "key" Office Bearers will consist of the President, the Vice President(s), the Secretary and the Treasurer and in the case of larger organisations, a paid Executive Officer. In their various roles, the objectives of the Office Bearers is to collectively work towards the operation, promotion and development of their organisation while individually, they each have a distinct and important role.

PRESIDENT.

The President is the cornerstone from which the organisation operates and grows. As the leader of the executive group, the President provides the strength and direction needed to keep the organisation on a firm footing.
In recent times, there has been a strong move towards a truly professional approach in Sports Administration. A successful organisation demands strong leadership. The President will preside at all meetings. IN his absence, the Vice-President presides. Where both are absent, the meeting elects a Chairman for that meeting from amongst their numbers. The President shall ensure that all rules are observed in their entirety and he will generally further the aims and objects of the organisation. He may exercise a deliberate vote on any question in issue and in the case of a deadlock, the President shall have the deciding vote.

VICE PRESIDENT.

The Vice President usually has a slightly more passive role than that of the President. However, it is again essential for the Vice President to be a person of strong character and the possessor of leadership qualities. The Vice President deputises for the President in the vent of his absence and at other times to relieve the President of some of his onerous duties. In many organisations, the Vice President is the heir apparent to the Presidency by virtue of the rules of most organisations which require that occupancy of the key positions be limited to a fixed term—generally between one and six years.

SECRETARY.

The Secretary's task is often a most demanding one and it requires a person who possesses a large element of organisational ability, as well as a lot of spare time. The Secretary's duties include the preparation of the agenda for meetings, the preparation of minutes of meetings and the preparation of all correspondence.

3. TREASURER'S ACCOUNTING SYSTEMS.

The Treasurer occupies an important position in any organisation by virtue of his role as financial adviser. He is responsible for the preparation and presentation of the financial statements of the organisation and must be fully informed as to the financial position at any given time. The Treasurer is often responsible for compliance with certain statutory requirements under the Companies Act or the Co-operatives Act, the Registered Clubs Act and in addition, he must furnish regular returns to the State Treasury where the Organisation receives revenue through the use of Poker Machines. IN general, the Treasurer's responsibilities shall be to:

Open a suitable banking account for all monetary dealings of the organisation.

Receive all monies of the organisation and promptly deposit them in the organisation's banking account.

Furnish financial statements on a regular monthly basis to the meetings of the organisation.

Submit the organisation's accounts to the Auditor for audit. All cheques drawn on the account must be signed by at least two authorised officers. The Treasurer is empowered to give a valid receipt for all monies received on behalf of the organisation. He will advise the organisation in respect of investments.

4. FINANCIAL PLANNING.

How much is it going to cost to run the Club for the year? These sums should not be too difficult if you have an efficient Treasurer who has kept actual expenditure records of previous years. Basically, expenses would be pitched at the same level of activity as last year with an adjustment this year for inflation. You then add in additional amounts if you are to increase your level of activity this year. You include the amounts for expansion of facilities. Budgets should never be that difficult to prepare. **Remember that it is usually 20% of the items, which represent 80% of the cost.** What you finish up with is a total cost of achieving your objectives for the year. Then comes the question—where are you going to get the money from? It is very important to be positive in this area. Here is a list possible sources of funds for a **sporting organisation**.

- **Affiliation Fees.**
- **Member's Subscriptions.**
- **Membership for Life.**
- **Poker Machines/Fruit Machines.**
- **Levies.**
- **Council Loans.**
- **Department of Sport and Recreation Grants.**
- **Banks.**
- **Commercial Sponsorship.**
- **Debentures.**
- **Gate Takings.**
- **Marketing of Products bearing Club's logo.**
- **Sundry Fund Raising.**

To elaborate briefly on each of these sources of income:

A AFFILIATION FEES.

Usually affiliation fees are payable by the various Clubs or Districts within the State to meet the promotion, development and administration costs of the State body. Affiliation fees are usually paid on a per capita basis.

B MEMBER'S SUBSCRIPTIONS.

Member's Subscriptions should meet the essential operating costs of a club. Many clubs are reluctant to increase member's subscriptions. **In a period in which inflation exceeds 10% per annum, operating costs are increasing and it follows that member's subscriptions should also.** If this is not done, a large and invariably unpopular increase will eventually have to be made. It is much better for all concerned to **have a steady annual increase in member's fees** rather than an infrequent big jump. **If members are getting value for their money, they will not often quibble.**

C MEMBERSHIP FOR LIFE.

This is a relatively new concept of obtaining funds. It is simply the offer of membership for life in return for the payment of a lump sum calculated to represent a number of years annual subscription at today's prices. **Upon payment of the lump sum**, the member is no longer liable to pay an annual subscription for the rest of his life. The number of members, to whom the offer of membership for life is made, is governed by the amount of finance required. It will usually be offered on a first-in first-served basis. **This is a cheap form of finance, which can produce relatively large sums for specific income producing purposes.**

D POKER MACHINES/FRUIT MACHINES.

Many clubs generate large sums from poker or fruit machines! This form of entertainment **is often the largest income producer for a club**. Poker/Fruit machines are subject to State Treasury regulations requiring registration of machines, payment of licence fees and often payment of a turnover tax. Despite these controls and taxes

E LEVIES.

Under its Articles, rules or By-Laws, a Club may have the power to impose a levy on its members. The decision to impose a levy is not one to be taken lightly by club administrators—**a levy is rarely regarded as a popular form of raising funds** and care should be taken to communicate the purposes for which the funds are to be used.

F COUNCIL LOANS.

In certain circumstances, **Councils will make available or arrange loan funds at reasonable rates of interest**. This area should be fully explored—what you are looking for is **relatively inexpensive long-term finance without having to produce security. The Council will often act as guarantor. It is up to you to acquaint yourself with the finance facilities available from your local council.**

DEPARTMENT OF SPORT AND RECREATION GRANTS.

Department of Sport and Recreation provides grants for a wide variety of purposes, which include the promotion, **and development of sport at all levels**. It is in the interests of each one of us to become fully informed of the types of grants available and the procedures required to obtain such grants. A phone call or a letter will be sufficient to obtain full details.

BANKS.

One of the problems of obtaining a bank loan is that the **Manager often requires a guarantee**. With most Clubs generally located on Crown land, **they may not have**

the assets to offer as security. If that does not apply to your organisation, well and good—you can obtain a bank loan. But here a word of caution—**a bank loan is a debt—it has to be repaid**. There is a periodic interest bill and the day of reckoning does come **when the principal has to be repaid. It is risk finance**. You should not really borrow from a bank unless the money will be used in a venture, which will generate income to service the loan.

A bank loan should not be used just to maintain existing facilities. It should be used to effect additions and improvements, which will **enhance the income earning potential of the Club**. If you abide by this rule, then the debt finance will not be a burden to the Club. On the question of security, as mentioned earlier that this can present a problem. **Some clubs where this problem has been overcome by a group of members offering personal guarantees. For example, a Club say borrows £10,000 from the bank, secured by a guarantee of £1,000 from each of 10 members** (personal guarantees do have to be watched very carefully, but with a reasonable limit and the funds being used for income producing purposes, **you may find the members willing to act as guarantors**.)

COMMERCIAL SPONSORSHIP E.G. SMALL BUSINESS & MANUFACTURERS.

If a Club is finding it difficult to promote or maintain the running of it's sport, it could be time to **seek the aid of a sponsor**. (Many companies will provide sponsorship if they are approached in a business-like manner and there is some commercial benefit to be derived from sponsorship of the particular sport!) Before an approach is made to a company on the subject of sponsorship, you would do well to examine the efficiency of our operation. Many clubs seek sponsorship **as the easy way out—as a cover for poor management**! Fortunately, this is not always the case, but it does happen. Commercial sponsorship can be a lucrative source of income provided your organisation can demonstrate to **the sponsor that he will gain media coverage for his product through involvement with your sport**.

DEBENTURES.

This is an interesting form of funding. A form of **borrowing from members repayable when the member leaves the Club or after a certain amount of time**. It is difficult to the levy I mentioned earlier in that the **debenture borrowing is eventually repaid**. The levy has a sense of compulsion and therefore can only be of a relatively small amount!

GATE TAKINGS (AS A SOURCE OF INCOME).

This source of income varies greatly depending upon the popularity of the particular sport.

MARKETING OF PRODUCTS BEARING THE CLUB LOGO.

In some of the more popular better organised sports, administrators are actually engaged in the marketing of clothing and equipment bearing the **Club Logo**. This can certainly be a lucrative source of income although there is often a need to purchase the product in large quantities.

SUNDRY FUND RAISING.

This is a convenient title describing non-specific sources of income although in practice, clubs would do well to apply the income for specific projects. This is not **always possible but suggest specific purpose fund raising for this reason**. If you are running a series of say, social functions, you will find the organisers more highly motivated than if the money was merely going into general revenue. The people behind the **social unit will have a goal to work towards.** They will then see something **tangible for their efforts.** This is a very important point when calling upon **volunteers on sub-committees** to work hard to raise money. They must see a distinct purpose for it—then they have a better chance of selling it if they can **communicate this purpose to potential customers**.

FEES.

The value of this funding source is obvious—**it does not have an interest cost and it does not have to be repaid**. In our financial planning, it is a little difficult to predict because the ultimate result depends upon **the enthusiasm and willingness of some hard workers**. The motivation of these people must never be lost sight of and they must be **appropriately rewarded**.

PROFESSIONALISM

5. BUDGETING.

Now is the time to match the costs with income. You must be realistic in your planning. In most cases, your first effort may **result in a cash shortfall** if your costs are greater than your income. At this stage, you must not take the easy way out and revise your goal—your vision of where you want the club to go. **You must go back through the figures and try to see where the extra money can be found!** Most of you, in drawing up budgets are pretty conservative—you tend to over estimate the costs and to underestimate the income. It gives you a feeling of security! That is all very well but really, what you want is **an honest budget—one which is realistic and attainable** and one which **stimulates your performance**—NOT a budget which acts as a governor and impedes your prospects of achievement. Your original objective for the Club should only be altered as a last resort. Hopefully, you have somebody, preferably the Chief Executive, who can see the whole picture, who can distinguish the wood from the trees and can take appropriate courses of action.

6. CASH FLOW.

Having established the **Objectives of the Club** and how much you are going to get there in financial terms, you must realise that **cash is the name of the game from thereon in. You must be able to meet your financial commitments when they fall due**. Therefore your twelve-month plan must be divided into monthly cash flows. A cash flow statement is simple—you commence with your opening balance, add your expected receipts and deduct your expected payments, so finishing off with your expected bank balance at the end of the month. This forecasting task must be done—the timing of your receipts and payments will vary during the year. If we prepare for the year projected cash flow statements, you come up with two important facts—the months you are going to be short of cash and the months you are going to have surplus cash. The months in which you are going to be short of cash must be anticipated so that you can take the appropriate action well in advance to tide you over this period. There is no value in waiting until you can't pay the bills and then wondering what you will do. **You must take a professional approach**. Any businessman worth his salt prepares projected statements of cash flow. Anticipating periods in which the club will be short of cash, you can then go along to the bank manager and obtain temporary accommodation. He will be delighted if you turn up with a projected cash flow statement. In these circumstances, he will be more than prepared to help you. Furthermore, your own committee need not be pessimistic when cash is down, if the plan shows quite clearly that within a month or two, the Club has more cash coming in than going out and therefore, the bank balance will look better.

EXAMINE A CASH FLOW STATEMENT

7. FINANCIAL CONTROL.

In financial control, you are concerned with monitoring your performance against the plan. **In financial terms, there is no sense in waiting until the end of the year to see how you have fared. You must continually monitor your financial position. You must monitor monthly performance**—compare what your income and expenses have actually been against what you thought they would have been. The point is, you must pick up any danger signals as quickly as possible and take appropriate action. There is no sense in having the control points too far apart, otherwise you could be in considerable difficulty before you realise it. What you're really talking about then is **periodically checking actual with budget, your actual cash-in for the month with actual cash-out for the month with budgeted cash-in**

and cash-out for the month. To put it in simple language, you will end up square, in front or behind. If you are behind, you have to decide where the problem exists. A small departure from budget does not matter—a significant departure does.

SUCCESSFUL ADMINISTRATION

8. FORWARD PLANNING.

You need to have a financial plan and dealt with in the manner in which you set out to achieve your objectives for the year. Now you will go a little beyond that point and deal with future planning—what you propose to achieve over the next, say, **three years!** In this respect, your approach is not unlike that adopted for the current year; however you must estimate your capital expenditure, your personnel growth and be able to assess the income needed to meet the additional costs. Certain basic rules can be applied as follows:

The club must have adequate capital.
The liquidity of the Club must be assumed at all times or it will be unable to meet its commitments.
Borrowing should be moderate and within the capacity to repay on due dates. This may take one of the forms discussed earlier but bank overdraft should be held in reserve to meet unforeseen emergencies.
Finance should be sought on the cheapest terms but in balance with other liabilities and avoiding commitments, which may be disastrous, if the club suffers adversity.
Capital expenditure should be programmed ahead and finance provided specifically either by capital or long-term borrowing so that working capital is not denuded.

STATUTORY OBLIGATIONS.

Administrators of **sporting organisations** have **certain statutory obligations** and it is well for each one of you to be aware of your responsibilities in this regard. In many cases, **sporting administrators** fall under the **umbrella** of the **Companies Act, the Co-operatives Act and the Registered Clubs Act** as well as certain **State Treasury regulations**. Under the Companies Act, sporting administrators may have responsibilities by virtue of their role **as a Director (specifically a registered company.)**

MASTERCLASS

Coaching Manua Official Accreditations:

Galactic Soccer/Football

Professional Secrets Revealed

Bert Holcroft Acc III Coach Northern and Southern Hemisphere

Professional Coaching Accreditations

Academy of Soccer/Football Excellence

Résumé Galactic Soccer/Football Courses

a) Pre Requisite Certificated and Accreditations Levels for Coaches + Players + Referees + Interested Parties who Participate In Pro Football, Football 2007 Course

b) Certificated Curriculum + Syllabus + Seminars

c) Eight Levels of Certificated Accreditation Pre Amble of Accreditation Levels

1) Level VI:—Master Coach to International Standard
2) Level V:—Football Professional Coaching Senior Standard
3) Level IV:—Football League of Members Senior Standard
4) Level III:—Football League of Associated Clubs Amateur

The above **Senior Accredited Coaches** must be held responsible for Organising and Implementing Coaching Seminars to improve Personal Proficiency in Coaching + Organising + Playing Standard, at all ages, **(7s to Senior),** Levels of Player participation in the game of **Soccer/Football.**

21ST CENTURY FUTURISTIC SOCCER/FOOTBALL
Academy of Excellence
Coaching and Fitness Revelations

Foreword, Administration, Coaching Techniques,

Fitness Grids and Drills (i—xxv)

Contents

Sections	Pages
1. Modes of Fitnesss	1-18
2. New Mode of Stretching Techniques	19-26
3. Principles & Applications	27-47
4. Weight Training Grids and Drills	48-64
5. Coaching Skills	65-78
6. Upgraded Soccer Techniques	79-87
7. Sports Psycology applied	88-94
8. Sports Nutrition	95-105
9. Somatograph	106-114
10. Fitness Revelations	115-138
#. Authors Accreditations	139-141

FUTURISTIC COACHING SOCCER/FOOTBALL

DEDICATION

To **My Wife Margo** who was a constant supporter plus contributor to every page in this **Book**, (which would never have reached the Publishers, without **Margo's Persistence**). She has always championed the underprivileged wannabe footballer who dream to play **Soccer/Football**, hoping to achieve a **Professional Status**, as a player. It was **Margo's Insistence**, that we penned this book.

This resulted in producing **"Soccer Revelations" . . . Coaching Book**.

We hope that the **"Secret revelations"** exposed in our book will be the catalyst to help these dreams become a reality.

We wish to share our expert knowledge of **"Coaching + Fitness + Technical Proficiencies"**, plus our **"Coaching Secrets"**, to any interested participant who, is ambitious enough to attain a **"Professional Status"** to the highest level of **"International"**, Representing the Country of their Birth.

Loving Husband Bert

Introduction

PROGRAMMING THE BODY FOR SUCCESS

MENTAL IMAGE TRAINING (M.I.T.)

BERT HOLCROFT

This equates with Conceptual and Perceptual imagery, facilitating the five disciplines of sporting participation and reaction to **Stress and Pressure Situations.**

1. Sports Psychology (Mind and Body).
2. Sports Physiology (Energy Facilitation).
3. Basic Game Disciplines (Visual Reactions).
4. Academic Disciplines (Learning Process).
5. Skill and Technical (Disciplines).

These functional proficiency disciplines should co-ordinate with the physiology, i.e. the **"Nine Levels"** of accepted fitness.—**Plateaux, optimum fitness levels, 9 disciplines** and the acquirement of the same.

"Perception or Conceived Perceptions" require perceived knowledge of **A. Object, B. It's Presence, C, Space and Time and D. Direction and Elevation,** derived and perceived from past learning and conceived from participation and experience gained in actual contesting the game of your choice **at the highest level** under pressure situations. Experiences gained are assessed for their **Technical Proficiency and Efficiency, i.e. A. Correct Movements** of the fundamental skill, **B. Bio—Mechanically** and Functionally, **C. Correction Drills** are initiated if required. **Conceived Perception**is gained by teaching and facilitating a learning process of correct movement patterns. These patterns are gained by repetitive technical **related drills** relating to **Personal Variables** in pressure **Orientated Situations. These Personal Variables** which relate to skill patterns and the energy systems are facilitated by Perceptual Images and Motor Nerve Impulses, which create an efficient "Engram System". These stored Motor Engrams respond to Automated Response impulse reaction to Elite Participants under Pressure Situations.

MOTOR ENGRAMS NEUROMUSCULAR MODES OF SKILLS—VARIABLES

1. **Speed Patterns** (Acceleration and Deceleration).
2. **Visual Response** (Focus and Direction).
3. **Visual Perceptions** (Direction, Space and Time).

Engrams: Perceptions and Interpretations

Determines safety plays, risk taking, skill choice and reaction selection under **Pressure Situations, Kinaesthetic awareness and extra dimensional awareness are pre-requisite** to improve personal proficiencies and to ensure facilitation of the engram system to produce the relevant "Skill Technique" requirement.

PROGRAMMING THE MIND FOR SUCCESS

ANALYSIS OF PSYCHO CYBERNETICS

5 Levels of Psychological Facilitation.

1.	Awareness	Span (100%) optimal
2.	Attention	Span (4 to 8 mins)
3.	Concentration	Span (100%)
4.	Tolerance (Controlled Aggression)	Levels (100%)
5.	Total Commitment	Levels (100%)

The Energy and Fatigue Syndrome is affected by these **5** psychological facilitations. These functional capacities are initiated by **Psychological Neuromuscular Response.** A second stage of **Fatigue** syndrome falls mainly in the **Psychological Categories,** which effects performance. The following reactions afterwards and accompanied with **Physical Fatigue** are these related **Psychological (2nd Stage)** fatigues, which initiates in the first place and prolongs **Physical Fatigue.**

The Second Stage Fatigues are:

A. **Emotional Fatigue.**
B. **Mental Fatigue.**
C. **Technical Fatigue.**

The Emotional Fatigue (A), which is triggered by **Unforced Error Situations** and **Like**, resorts a feeling of **Embarrassment and Inadequacies, Fear and Intimidation.**

The Mental Fatigue (B) relates to the nervous system and disengages **(C) The Neuro Muscular System**, which produces Technical Deficiencies. These physiological disturbances delay the concept of **Spatial or Temporal Summation** of an **Action Potential**, causing inhibitions of the skill technical procedures. These **2 types of 2nd Stage** fatigue or not **Physiological** but **Psychological** responses and all mainly caused by self-initiated and inflicted reactions, **emotional anger** etc. **The Technical Fatigue** is of course the most depressing fatigue of all. This fatigue is once again **self inflicted**. The main cause of **Technical Fatigue** is the lack of skill facilitation of **Basic Technical Requirements**.

NEUROMUSCULAR FATIGUE SYNDROME:

STRESS AND PRESSURE SITUATIONS

To reduce the pressure and stressful situation, cultivate the ability to reduce the

demand **you place on yourself.** Your imagination of what you expect of yourself as an **individual player or a certain group of players**, even the **rest of the team.** Your visualisation or interpretation of level of **intensity or urgency** could result in an **over burden situation** on your self or your team mates. To fulfil this **over demand**, you can and **must reduce pressure situations** placed on yourself or your team, by keeping an **open mind** and a **flexible attitude**, regarding **Trade-Offs** in **pressure or stressful situations.**

BASIC STRESS PERCENTAGES

Basic Principles relating to **Elite Conditioning** also relate to the amount of **stress** you put on your body, **specifically Cardio-Respiratory and Physiological, i.e. muscles and joints** of exercise **if** performed at a level under **65%** of your **V02 Maximal Capacity,** Your body does not **adapt to stress.** The **activity** will not be of **sufficient Intensity** for an adaptive process to be **facilitated or occur**. If the type of **stress** is not of an exact nature, depending on which component of fitness you strive to improve, the desired level of fitness will **not be achieved**.

ELITE ATHLETE

Tangibles and Intangibles

Levels of performance in **sport participation** are mainly accredited to and

determined by **theTangibles—the known** and**the Intangibles—the unknown**. The tangible assets are easily assessed through **perceptual vision**. It is the **unknown** or **intangibles**, i.e. the **invisible** and **immeasurable** actions and reactions relating to interpretation of a **functional activity** Problems, **psychological and emotional phases** stimulate reaction, i.e. **pride, attitude, determination, commitment and dedication** levels are listed amongst these **intangibles**.

Amongst the most notable **intangible** Phases are strengths and weaknesses under **pressure situations**. The **unknown response, i.e. anger, aggression, fear or exhilaration, satisfaction, discipline and reliability**are also levels of **psychological stimulants or depressants**through **tension or stress-related confrontations**. These **intangibles**, which relate directly with **sport participation** and reaction to **pressure situations or frustration and stress-related situations** triggered by **bio-chemical reaction,** relate to the **emotional plateaux.**If these **intangibles** produce **emotional and depressive reactions, the levels of fitness** and all of the **nine levels** of function produce **lowered responses** and facilitate the onset of **fatigue**. The effects of **concentration awareness and attention spans**are affected drastically, producing **unforced errors**, lack of **communication** and loss of **control**, particularly **infactions and discipline**. When the **tangible and intangible** are brought into **focus** and assessed, the athlete's **idiosyncrasies and characteristics** can be determined under **stressful and pressure situations**.

These **physiological disturbances** delay the concept of **Spatial Temporal Summation** of an **Action Potential,** causing inhibition of the **Skill Technical Procedure.**

INTRODUCTION TO MODERN CONCEPTS OF CHANGE, RELATING TO FITNESS

In Pro Mod Sport, emerging disciplines produce new scientific study of **Human movement:** (1) in the concept of **Bio-Mechanics** and (2) **Concepts of Psychological and Physiological Kinesiological Science of Human Movement relate to:**
- A. Neuronal Mechanisms, **i.e.** Perception and Motivation.
- B. Nine Components of Fitness for Elitism.
- C. Bio-Mechanical Process, **i.e.** to initiate and sustain.

Human Movements, i.e. Time, Distance, Space & Force Concepts relate to:
- 1st Human Movement Kinesiology
- 2nd Physiology and Bio-Mechanics.
- 3rd Mechanical Kinesiology.

Exercise Grids for Application and Facilitation of the **Nine Components** relating to **Optimum Fitness Exercise Physiology, Power and Levels of Intensity.**

ANALYSIS OF AN ELITE ATHLETE

Expounded, along with **Basic Disciplines and Obedience (M.I.P.—Mental Image Programming).**

FUNCTIONAL SPORTS—PHYSIOLOGY, ENCAPSULATING THE NINE LEVELS OF FITNESS.

1. Cardio-vascular.	2. Strength.	3. Power
4. Aerobic Capacity.	5. Endurance.	6. Flexibility.
7. Anaerobic.	8. Speed.	9. Agility.

Plus three levels of endurance.
- A. **Cardio-respiratory** endurance.
- B. **Local & Muscular** endurance.
- C. **Strength & Power** endurance.

During the three stages of skill facilitation:
- A. **Cognitive** initial knowledge
- B. **Association** learning capacity.
- C. **Autonomous** automatic functional capacity.

Mod Technical Skill Acquisition initiates Elitism in athletes.

MODERN SCIENTIFIC AND ACADEMICAL DISCIPLINES

Attitudes towards academic and scientific training are making radical inroads into the new modes of sport. This radical approach is now accepted as the norm. It is now recognised and accepted that **academic discipline** relates to more efficient and proficient facilitation of **upgraded technical components.** The accepted quest of science to **bisect and discern.** i.e. the **how and why,** the theoretical as well as practical, is perceived to determine a more acceptable learning process towards realisation that physiological awareness is a pre-requisite in acquiring **Scientific—Bio Mechanical and Kinesiological** knowledge, to facilitate modern training for **Elitism in Sport.**

PHILOSOPHY OF TRAINING (A-F)

With correct attitude, sacrifice and regular training. (A) Your body systems adapt to absorb more pressure and tension. (B) As your training increases in intensity temperament and perseverance are very important. (C) You have to accept the philosophy of Gradual Physical Adaptation in the Nine Levels of Fitness. (D) If you have considerable strength of will power, persistence and ample self-confidence, you will excel personally. (E) If you are mentally prepared for the most stressful of conditions (pressure etc.), good performance must follow. (F) If you have prepared well, both mentally and physically, good results should ensue.

ELITE FITNESS FOR SPORTING EXCELLENCE
By
ACCREDITED III COACH BERT HOLCROFT

PRINCIPLES AND APPLICATIONS TERMS AND DEFINITIONS. RELEVANT TERMS AND THEIR MEANING

1. **EQUILIBRIUM**—a state of balance as shown by a body which is static (stationary) in one position.
2. **FORCE**—the effort exerted by one body upon another by either a push or pull. It is impossible to have motion without force, although possible to have force without motion, e.g. gravity on a player standing still.
3. **MASS**—the amount of matter contained within an object. For our purposes, think of weight as being the same as man.
4. **SPEED**—the rate of change of position, i.e. from one point to another.
5. **VELOCITY**—the rate of change of position in a given direction.

6. **ACCELERATION**—the rate of change of velocity. If it Is gaining acceleration, it is said to be positive acceleration. If it is losing acceleration, then it is negative or deceleration.

7. **MOMENTUM**—the amount of motion in a moving body. It is the product of the body's mass and velocity (**MOMENTUM = MASS !VELOCITY**)and is often said to be the impetus gain by movement.

AEROBIC TRAINING.

To develop aerobic capacity, it is important to:
1. Use large muscle group activity, e.g. running, swimming.
2. Train continuously for at least 30 minutes in each session.
3. Train at least 3 times per week.
4. Train at an intensity, which will demand **60% to 85%**of maximum oxygen uptake **of your T.H.R—Age-related Target Heart Rate.**

Aerobic **capacity** may be developed through **continuous running, interval training, circuit training and circuit weight training.** The improvements which occur in maximum oxygen uptake with **aerobic training**will usually vary from **5 to 25%** depending on the initial fitness and the **intensity of training.**

Aerobic fitnessis important in all sports but is particularly important in sports, which require **high levels of endurance performance.**

AEROBIC POWER

PRINCIPLES OF EXERCISE—IMPORTANT COMPONENT

Before calling on cold muscles to perform sudden and vigorous activity, they should be warmed and loosened by a series of exercises designed to cover the whole body. Simple exercises and running activities are necessary to prepare the respiratory, circulatory and muscular systems of the body for strenuous activity to follow. Muscular contraction is most rapid and most powerful when the temperature of the muscle fibres is slightly higher than the normal body temperature. In this slightly warmed condition, the muscle viscosity is lowered, the chemical reactions of contraction and recovery are more rapid, and the circulation is improved. **"The heat of muscular contractions thus tend to improve the condition of the muscles for further work."**

CALISTHENICS FOR WARM-UP ABDOMINALS

Exercise
Sit-ups.
Upper Body.

Value of Exercise
Before Stretching
Works hip flexor & then abdominal muscles.

Component of Fitness
Mobility & Muscular Strength.

UPPER BODY

1. (8 stations x 20 reps)

SIT-UPS (BEND KNEES).

LOWER BODY

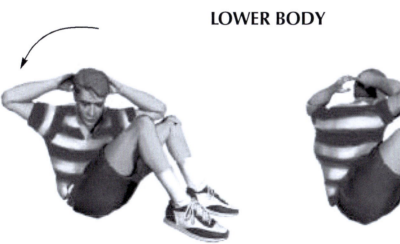

SIT-UPS

Side Stomach - (External Obliques).
These protect against internal injuries.

TWIST TO LEFT & RIGHT TOUCH KNEE WITH OPPOSITE ELBOW.

MOBILITY AND STRENGTH
DO NOT HOLD YOUR BREATH DURING EXERCISE

UPPER BODY

2. Push-ups

Increases strength and endurance in shoulders and chest muscles. Muscular strength and endurance.

PUSH-UPS.
STRENGTH &
ENDURANCE FOR
SHOULDERS AND CHEST.

LOWER BODY

3. Tucking High Jump

Provides exercise for heart and lungs, development of power in the legs and a mobility exercise for the spine and hips. Agility and mobility.

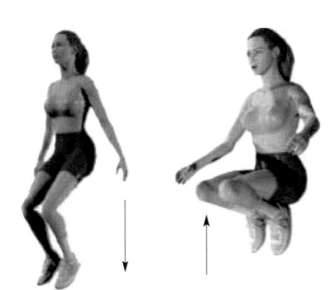

TUCKING HIGH JUMP
AGILITY AND MOBILITY
FOR THIGHS AND
LOWER BACK.

BREATHE NORMALLY DURING EXERCISE.

CALISTHENICS FOR WARM UP CIRCUIT
MINIMUM 20 REPETITIONS

LOWER BODY

4. Astride Jumping (Agility & Mobility)

This develops power in the legs and is a mobility exercise for the hips.

* Lift arms to shoulder level.

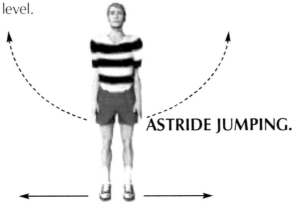

ASTRIDE JUMPING.

5. Squats (Lower Body)

Strengthens the thigh muscles. Muscular strength.

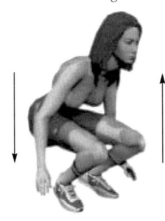

SQUATS
MUSCULAR STRENGTH FOR HIPS AND THIGHS.

6. Burpees (Upper & Lower Body)

For stamina and suppleness, endurance and agility.

BURPEES - 4 COUNT - CYCLIT

1   2   3   4   1

FACTORS INFLUENCING SPORTS PERFORMANCE:

Flexibility: Stretching Exercises.

Stretching after warm-up (not before warming up) is an essential factor to prevent muscle injury when intensity is increased. Joint flexibility is Important in all sports to maximise performance and to prevent soft tissue injury. Flexibility exercises should also be performed to compensate for the shortening effect which repetitive exercise has on working muscles.

The athlete should precede stretching exercises with large muscle group warm—up activity and should stretch all muscle groups, particularly those engaged in the sport. Pre-training for contact sports must include **(Compact-impact-Collision Drills).**

Rules of Stretching

1. **Never bounce when you are stretching,** just stretch to a comfortable position and hold it. When you feel your muscles relax in that position, stretch a bit more.
2. **Do not hold your breath when stretching.** Exhale as you bend forward and breathe naturally and rhythmically whilst holding the stretch.
3. **Hold your stretches for between 15-30 seconds.**

JUMPING INTO PLYO-DYNAMICS POWER.

Plyo-dynamics, i.e. "metrics" = measurable and "plyo" applied, increases is a new mode of scientific exercises relating to exercise physiology, a new component to relate to mod formulae and variables of the nine components of elite fitness.

Plyo-dynamics drillsare specifically to link strength with speed of movement to encompass training programs. **Power Plyo-dynamics** is defined as exercises that enable a muscle to reach maximum strength in the shortest possible time. Speed, strength and agility are related to power. **Plyo-dynamics** is the catalyst or the mechanics of power. **Plyo-dynamics** facilitate power.

TECHNICAL PROFICIENCIES ILLUSTRATED

1. Speed Drills: Plyo-Dynamics
Drill No.1—High Knees

Value, develops the muscles for a fast, long stride and adds flexibility in the hamstrings.

**Pump arms vigorously.
Do not pump hands
above shoulder level.**

SET	EACH LEG
1st	20
2nd	50
3rd	100

2. Drill No. 2—Heel-ups

Value, develops strength in the hamstring and active flexibility in quadraceps.

TAP HEELS WITH HANDS

SET	EACH LEG
1st	20
2nd	50
3rd	100

3. Power Related Drills
Drill No. 3 Bounding

SET	EACH LEG
1st	20
2nd	50
3rd	100

SPRINT 20 YARDS
AFTER EACH
DRILL.

TRAINING TECHNIQUES
COMBINE DRILLS WITH 20-METRE SPRINTS

4. Jumps

ACTION:
Jump continuously, reaching with alternating hands and trying to reach the object on every jump.

A. Vary number of jumps.

B. Alternate hand reach.

C. Stand jumps.

D. Alternate single jumps.

E. 3 ¥ step, run and jump.

5. With Change-of-Direction Sprint

ACTION:
Do two-footed hops over the row of cones; as you are clearing the last cone, your partner points to one of the far cones; sprint to that cone immediately upon landing from the last hop.

6. Hurdle Jumps

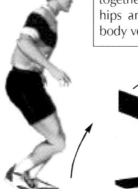 

ACTION:
Jump forward over the barrier with feet together. Movement comes from the hips and knees, be sure to keep the body vertical and straight.

1. Vary number of hurdles.
2. Space & Distance.
3. Sprints on completion of exercises -
4. Forward – diagonal and lateral after each drill.
5. Multi-Directional Field Sprints.

PLYO DYNAMIC FIELD DRILLS
COMBINE WITH 20 METRE SPRINTS

7. Alternate Single-Leg Hops

ACTION:
Push off with the leg you are standing on and jump forward landing on the same leg. Use a strong leg swing to increase length of jump and strive for height off each jump.

8. Alternate Leg Bounding

ACTION:
Bound from one foot as far forwards as possible, using the other leg and arms to cycle in the air for balance and to increase forward momentum.

9. Alternate Hop From Side To Side

ACTION:
Jump from one line to the other in a continuous forward motion for 10 metres, always taking off and landing on the same foot.

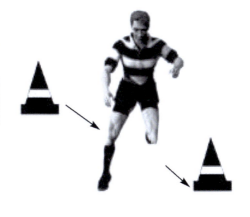

8 x 5 (20 METRE) ZIG-ZAG DRILL COMBINED WITH 20 METRE SPRINTS FORWARD, DIAGONAL & LATERAL – (5 TO LEFT) x (5 TO RIGHT) x ALTERNATED SPRINTS AFTER EACH DRILL.

MOD PLYO-DYNAMICS—AGILITY

10. Stand-jump over tackling bags.

After each each exercise, sprint 20 metres to the cone and return.

11. Ski Power Drills.

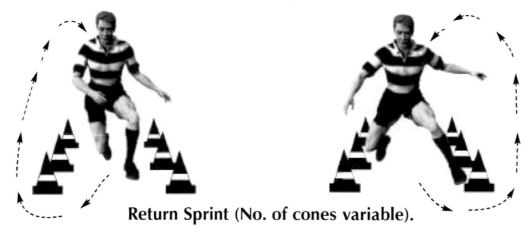

Return Sprint (No. of cones variable).

12. Stand-Jump Over Cones (vary number and size of cone).
Sprint 20 Metres after each exercise.
Stand-Jump – Vary number of jumps.

Drill. Sprint 20 Metres Around Cone

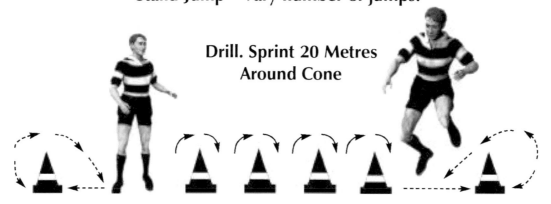

7-POSITIONS—EXERCISE PROGRAM
ALL SPORTS STRETCHING

AEROBIC TRAINING

To develop aerobic capacity, it is important to:
1. Use large muscle group activity, e.g. running, swimming
2. Train continuously for at least 30 minutes in each session.

TRAINING ZONES

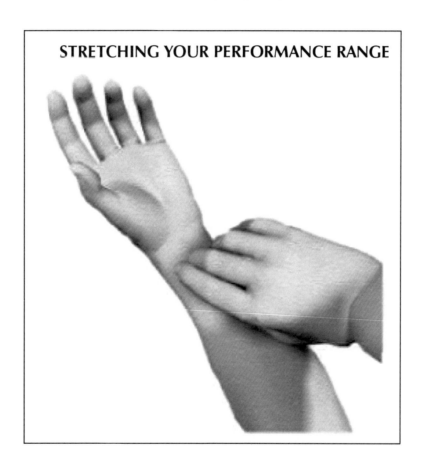

STRETCHING YOUR PERFORMANCE RANGE

Age-related target heart rates—maintain at least 60% of your target heart rate.

Count your pulse or artery beats for six seconds, then multiply by ten for H.B.P.M. After warm up, continue to monitor your H.B.P.M. every few minutes. Try to stay within the target training zone. Either work up to it or if you exceed the training zone, slow your exercise down until your H.B.P.M. falls into target training zone.

Example: Beats 10 in 6 seconds = 6x10 = 60 beats per minute.

SECTION 2

COACHING KNOWLEDGE
FITNESS AND TRAINING REGIMES

TEST CHARTS
SEE SPEED GUIDELINES FOR SPORT

> **IMPORTANT**
>
> A warm-up period is essential before commencing any programme. Stretch and limber-up all the major joint areas. The same warm-up routine should also be used for a cool-down.

REACHING A PEAK
BIO-MECHANICS & PHYSIOLOGY

A. WITH *NUTRITIONAL* GUIDELINES.
B. *STRETCHING* EXERCISE TECHNIQUES.
C. *JOINT & MUSCULAR* FUNCTION TESTING.
D. MOD *PLYO-DYNAMIC* DRILLS.
E. ADVANCED *WEIGHT-TRAINING* GRIDS & CHARTS.
F. AGE-RELATED *TARGET HEART RATE* CHARTS.

PEAK FITNESS—SOMATOGRAPH CHARTS

COACHING KNOWLEDGE

THE "NEW MODE" PRE-SCREENING AND STRETCHING.

MUSCULAR FUNCTION TESTS.

INTRODUCTION: BASIC STRETCH.

DEFINITION: PROCEDURES, MUSCLES.

SPORTS ACTIVITIES AND APPROPRIATE EXERCISES—M.F.T., i.e. MUSCULAR FUNCTION TEST.

FITNESS REGIME.

> **IMPORTANT**
>
> A warm-up period is essential before commencing any programme. Stretch and limber up all the major joint areas. The same warm-up routine should also be used for a cool-down.

NEW SPORT DIMENSIONS.

EXPANSIVE STRETCHING METHOD FOR RUGBY.

COACHING CO-ORDINATOR—BERT HOLCROFT.

MUSCLE FUNCTION TESTS

NEUROMUSCULAR FACILITATION OF APPLIED KINESIOLOGY

Facilitation of neuromuscular activity in human subjects refers to strength and endurance. Neuromuscular facilitation involves basic changes within the central nervous system that permits an individual to increase muscular performances, either concentrically or eccentrically. **Testing for muscular deficiency—M.F.T**—during the performance of **(maximum contractions)** should detect any **muscular weakness in joints, muscles and ligaments.** Principles upon which the testing method of increasing strength responses is based on an increasing range of motion through neuro muscular facilitation involves **the principles of maximum M.F.T. contraction against resistance.** (See charts with illustrations 1 to 12).

MUSCULAR FUNCTION TEST

M.F.T.—DEFINITIONS AND PROCEDURES

The method is a relatively new approach to athletes and in order to understand how it differs from traditional testing methods, the exercise sequence is necessary that the player comprehend a few simple definitions.

1. **Flexibility—range or extent of motion possible in given joint.**
2. **Strength—maximal amount of force that an individual can produce in one contraction.**
3. **Concentric contraction—muscular effort that results in joint movement, due to the shortening of the contracting muscle tissue.**
4. **Exerciser resists tester.**
5. **Tester resists exercise.**
6. **Concentric functional strengths.**
7. **Eccentric functional strength.**

PLYO-KINETIC PROGRAMME (A) & (B)

PLYO-DYNAMICS WITH PLYO-KINESTHETICS: NEW MOD WARM-UP TECHNIQUES

This program defines somatic facilitation using Plyo-dynamics and kinaesthetics to determine muscular function—strength and flexibility in co-operating **P.N.F. (Proprioceptive Neuromuscular Facilitation)** characteristics. Two people, as partners and as a team, go through a full résumé of resistant pressure-related exercises. **The protagonists are the prime movers in muscular function.** The antagonists are the controllers. Therefore, for this exercise, player **A** would act as the antagonist, player **B** would act as the protagonist. Player **A** would resist player **B** from contracting.

PLYO-KINETIC & PLYO-KINESTHETICS FUNCTION 2

PROPREOCEPTIVE NEUROMUSCULAR FUNCTION FACILITATION

1. **A resists B's movements.**
2. **B resists A's movements.**
3. **A resists B's concentric and eccentric function.**
4. **B resists A's concentric and eccentric function to create kinaesthetic reaction, i.e. joints and tendons, ligaments and muscles and nerves.**

Afferent and efferent facilitation through tension related motion. Player A reacts without **B's** knowledge in all aspects. **Concentric, eccentric contraction, relaxation, extension, flexion, abduction, abduction and circumduction**—interacted movements **(B)** reaction to resist all of the functions which are activated by his partner **(A)**.

MUSCLES & JOINTS-FUNCTIONAL TESTS
=(M.J.F.T.)—FOR A FULL STRETCH: (M.J.F.T.) TECHNIQUES
Positions to which M.J.F.T. is applied

23

MUSCLE FUNCTION TESTS

M.F.T.—DEFINITIONS AND PROCEDURES
ALL SPORTS—EXERCISE PROGRAM

M.F.T. i.e. MUSCULAR FUNCTION TEST

POSITIONS
FOUR WAYS FUNCTIONAL TESTING

7. Hamstring Stretch — FORWARD & DOWNWARD (HAMSTRINGS) LEFT & RIGHT LEG

8. Quadricep Stretch — FORWARD & BACKWARD (FRONT THIGH) LEFT & RIGHT LEG

9. Abductor Stretch (Vastus Internus) — INSIDE & OUTSIDE Groin Area OUTWARDS & INWARDS

FITNESS REGIME

CONCENTRIC & ECCENTRIC-MUSCLES & JOINTS-TEST LIGAMENTS & TENDONS

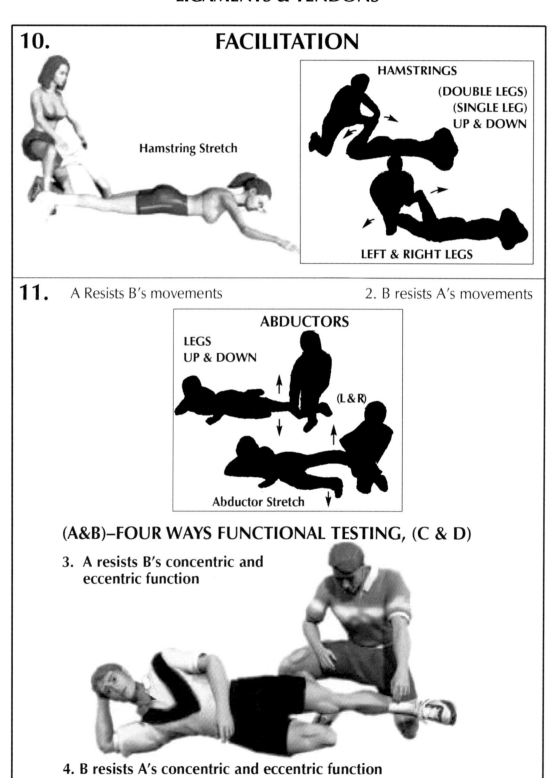

10. FACILITATION

Hamstring Stretch

HAMSTRINGS
(DOUBLE LEGS)
(SINGLE LEG)
UP & DOWN

LEFT & RIGHT LEGS

11. A Resists B's movements   2. B resists A's movements

ABDUCTORS
LEGS UP & DOWN
(L & R)
Abductor Stretch

(A&B)–FOUR WAYS FUNCTIONAL TESTING, (C & D)

3. A resists B's concentric and eccentric function

4. B resists A's concentric and eccentric function

SECTION 3

PEAK FITNESS SOMATOGRAPH CHARTS

COMPLETE GUIDE TO FITNESS AND TRAINING

TEST CHARTS

REACHING A PEAK:
SEE SPEED GUIDELINES

IMPORTANT

A warm-up period is essential before commencing any programme. Stretch and limber up all the major joint areas. The same warm-up routine should also be used for a cool-down.

TO FACILITATE SPORTS PARTICIPATION

WITH NUTRITIONAL GUIDELINES STRETCHING AND

MUSCULAR FUNCTION • TESTS • PLYO-DYNAMICS

WEIGHT TRAINING AND CHARTS

AGE-RELATED TARGET HEART RATE CHART

BY BERT HOLCROFT

PSYCHO CYBERNETICS

MIND COMPUTER PROGRAMMING

To assess and analyse the nine levels of physiological facilitations through Psychosomatic disciplines.

1. Awareness .... Span 100%
2. Attention .... Span 100%
3. Concentration ...... Span 100%
4. Tolerance .... Span 100%
5. Intensity .... Levels 100%
6. Responsibility.
7. Attitude .... Levels 100%
8. Application .... Levels 100%
9. Dedication .... Levels 100%

PSYCHOLOGY & PHYSIOLOGICAL ANALYSIS.

The above nine spans and levels Psychologically relate to second-stage physiological levels of neuromuscular fatigue syndromes, if **span levels are not maintained.**

PSYCHOLOGY AND PHYSIOLOGY RELATED TO SPORT PARTICIPATION

ASSESSMENT OF THE PSYCHO CYBERNETIC THEORY

This places great store in a player being an Information System, through additional input of correct information from teaching processed by the mind with further input from audial and visual informed practices. **The three phases of learning relate to:**

1. Cognitive, 2. Association and 3. Autonomative theories to achieve optimum personal achievements of proficiency of the skills required for elitism in sport. Your Psychological Function must be co-ordinated with your physiological plateaux to acquire this elitism. To achieve autonomative facilitation of technical soundness requires acknowledgement of the theory **"No one person can teach another person anything". You have to rely on the pupil's capacity to learn, i.e. absorb,** after providing the correct stimuli of technical proficiencies, for assimilation. To acquire these proficiencies requires the participant to produce the correct technical qualities to combine with psychological and physiological plateaux. **The two most important functions in the physiological facilitation relate to cardio-vascular and cardio-respiratory systems efficiency to record an average percentage of your age-improved target heart rate of 70% ˙ V02 maximum**to achieve this essential physiological facilitation, finds particular value in scientific training methods of the **Nine Levels of Fitness** to give you a progressive measurement of your achievements. Goals and targets must be set and achieved to combine and initiate an elite performance. **One must register 48 points on the Somatograph Certificate of fitness (see chart).**The starting requirement standard relates to your˙ **V02 maximum** Your respiratory systems ability to utilise oxygen of approximately **58.2 ml/kg—min,** i.e. to be able to record a **6-minute mile daily**with field testing to facilitate this **Physiological and Psychological Relationship, with reference to the four systems of elite levels of fitness.**

1. **Circuit Training**
2. **The Interval Training** . . . . with weights
3. **Integrating Aerobics** . . . . training with weights
4. **Alternate Muscular Function** . . . with weights

PHYSIOLOGY OF THRESHOLD TRAINING

(1)(V02-MAX)-(CARDIO-VASCULAR)-(CARDIO-RESPIRATORY) FIELD TRAINING

Select from 10 individual drills. Divide into (400 yards !8) exercise—Select from:

1. Acceleration . . . . Sprints.
2. Sustained . . . . Sprints.
3. Hollow . . . . Sprints.
4. Continuous . . . . Sprints.
5. Leg Speed . . . . Techniques.
6. Interval . . . . Runs.
7. Continuous Rhythmic Training.
8. Aerobic Intensity . . . . . Runs.
9. Aerobic Intensity . . . . . Splits.
10. An Aerobic Threshold Training.
    1. Warm-Up.   2. Stretch.   3. Activity.
    4. Cool-Down   5. Stretch

BE TECHNICAL PROFICIENT

ELITE FITNESS

TYPES OF TRAINING

1. Weight Training.
Progressive resistance exercise, which uses weights and repetitions to progressively increase the work done. Weight training is a very effective way to increase muscular strength, endurance and power, muscle mass and flexibility.

2. Circuit Training.
A circuit of well-chosen exercises which are performed in a specific sequence and aimed at developing specific components of physical fitness. Training may be against the clock and may use weight-training equipment to produce overload.

3. Interval Training.
A series of intensive bursts of physical activity, interspersed with intervals of physical activity of lower intensity. By modifying the distance, time, intensity and length of recovery period, specific training objectives can be achieved.

NINE COMPONENTS FOUR LEVELS
WITH FIVE INTENSITIES—(VO2MAX), AGE RELATED TARGET HEART RATE.

Circuit: In circuit training, not only does everything have to be done as fast as possible but correct technique in the execution of the work is absolutely essential. Otherwise the circuit training will be so much waste of time.

The Keeping of Times: The keeping of times of each individual's performance is of utmost importance, as this is the only way to measure improvement. The times should be recorded on a chart against each player's name and the date the time was set. If the chart is made out in columns, a player's subsequent times can be entered alongside one another and the rate of his improvement can readily be seen.

Exercise Selection: In the selection of exercises for a circuit, sequence is most important. One important principle of circuit training is the avoidance of local fatigue through the exercise of different parts of the body in turn. For example, the coach would not consecutively use arm exercises because performance of the second would suffer through arm fatigue engendered by the first.

A sound guide to the choice of the right types of exercise is the player's requirements on the field of play. In addition to required proficiency in the basic football skills, the player is subjected in body and mind to all kinds of stresses and strains in a match. To come through this efficiently, the player must have NINE components of fitness. These are:

1. **Agility.**
2. **Co-ordination.**
3. **Flexibility.**
4. **General endurance.**
5. **Muscular strength.**
6. **Muscular endurance.**
7. **Mobility.**
8. **Power.**
9. **Speed.**

The coach, aware of this, will choose exercises that will help to promote each of these components. The exercises are then put into proper sequence in the circuit, with care to ensure that successive routines will exercise different parts of the body.

The following shows which exercises are best for each component of fitness and the parts of the body they serve most beneficially.

SPECIFIC FIELD TRAINING FOR SPEED AND ENDURANCE

Speed Play or Fartlek Training: Personal Profile Fitness

Speed play or fartlek (a Swedish word meaning "speed play") training is said to be the forerunner of the interval training system. It involves alternating fast and slow running over natural terrain. It can be thought of as an informal interval-training program in that neither the work nor relief intervals are precisely timed. Furthermore, the proportions of fast and slow running are left entirely up to the runners as they feel the need or urge to develop them. Such a program will develop both aerobic and anaerobic capacities. An example of a training schedule for one workout using the fartlek method is as follows:

A 1. **Warm up by running easily for 5 to 10 minutes.**
    2. **Run at a fast steady speed over a distance of ¾ to 1¼ miles.**
    3. **Walk rapidly for 5 minutes.**
    4. **Practise easy running, broken by sprints of 65 to 75 yards, repeating until fatigue becomes evident.**

5. Run easily, injecting 3 to 4 swift steps occasionally.
6. Run at full speed uphill for 175 to 200 yards.
7. Run at a fast pace for 1 minute.
8. Finish the routine by running 1 to 5 laps around the track, depending on the distance run in competition.

Another example of a fartlek workout would be:

B
1. Jog 10 minutes as a warm-up.
2. 4 minutes' brisk callisthenics.
3. 1 to 2 x ¾ t o 1¼ miles at a fast steady pace that might be described as ¾ full speed. Walk 5 minutes after each.
4. 4 to 6 x 150-yard acceleration sprints (jog 50 yards, stride 50 yards, sprint 50 yards and walk 50 yards after each.)
5. 4 to 6 x 440 yards at slightly faster than jogging effort. Jog 440 yards after each.
6. Walk 10 minutes.
7. Continuous slow-running for 2 minutes.
8. Walk 5 minutes.
9. 8 to 12 x 110 yards at 1½ to 2½ seconds slower than best effort, jogging 110 yards after each. Walk 5 minutes.
10. Jog 1 mile as a cool-down.

Sprint Training.

This type of training is used by sprinters to develop speed (ATP—PC) and muscular strength. Here, repeated sprints at maximal speed are performed. **About 6 seconds are required to accelerate to maximum speed from a static start.** Therefore, the sprinter should run at least **60 yards** on each sprint in order to experience moving at top speed. **Also, because each sprint should be performed at top speed, recovery between repetitions must be complete.**

Interval Sprinting.

Interval sprinting is a method of training whereby an athlete alternately **sprints 50 yards and jogs 60 yards for distances up to 3 miles.** For example, over 440 yards, the sprinter would perform **four 50-yard sprints, jogging 60 yards after each; repeat 12 times.** Because of fatigue setting in after the first few sprints, the athlete will not be able to run **subsequent sprints at top speed.** This factor, plus the relatively long distances covered per training session **(up to 3 miles)**, makes this type of training system suitable for the **development of the aerobic system.**

PHYSICAL TRAINING: SPEED FOR SPORT

Acceleration Sprints.

As the name implies, acceleration sprints involve a gradual increase in running speed from **jogging to striding and finally to sprinting.** The jogging, striding and sprinting intervals **may consist of 50-yard, 110-yard or 120-yard segments.** In each case, recovery should consist of walking. For example, **a sprinter may jog 50 yards, stride 50 yards, sprint 50 yards, walk 50 yards and then repeat.** Because recovery between repetitions is nearly complete, **this type of training develops speed and strength.** Also, it is a good method to use in cold weather since the runs are graduated from easy to hard, **thus lessening the chances of muscular injury.**

Hollow sprints.

Hollow sprints involve the use of two sprints interrupted by a hollow period of either jogging or walking. These sprints are performed in repeats; one repetition might involve **sprinting 60 yards, jogging 60 yards, and then walking 60 yards.** Similar intervals might include distances up to but **not beyond 220 yards.**

Application of Training Methods for Contact Sports.

A summary of the prescription content for the various training methods is presented in Table **1. Although the prescriptions are for Rugby Players,** they may be applied to other sports and activities with minimal adaptations. **For example, acceleration sprints, hollow sprints, interval-training and sprint-training methods might be modified for the Rugby players as follows:**

1. Prescribe sprint distances of only 40-50 yards.

2. Prescribe backward and lateral running.

3. Prescribe stop-and-go sprinting (i.e., the runner sprints for 5 yards, then stops and reaches out to touch the ground, then sprints 5 more yards, reaches out and touches the ground, and so on, for a total of 40-50 yards).

ANAEROBIC EXERCISE

Repetition Sprints: Anaerobic Fitness.

The programme below consists of two methods of training—**(acceleration sprints and interval sprints).** You may wish to attempt this programme by yourself or you may find that your coach or trainer is giving you enough of this type of training pre-season anyway.

Acceleration Sprints: Concentrics.

Use a football field divided into five-metre intervals. Build up speed for the first **20** metres, sprint the second **20**metres, ease up over the next **20**metres. Rest for **15-30**seconds (as long as it takes to recover)—remember, you are aiming at quality training.

Interval Sprints.

These are sprints done at maximum speed for a certain distance, followed by a specified recovery time. After each set, recover before the next set is attempted.

Monitoring Heart Rate.

Pulse rate =V02MAX—Target heart rate.
Subtract your age from 220 =—H/R.
Calculate 60-65% of this number =—H/R.
This determines your warm up/cool down =-H/R.
Fitness zone: Calculate 75-85% of your predicted heart rate to determine your Intensity Levels.

Pre-season, Season Fitness and Conditioning Programme.

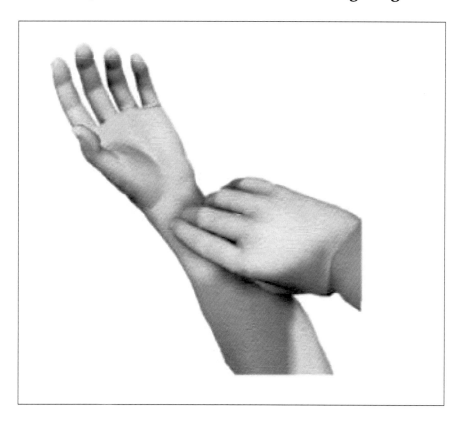

1. SPEED PRINCIPLES.

The prime movers and assistant prime movers, i.e. leg musculature used in skill activity and sprint training should be developed to an optimum level of functional activity **(aerobic and anaerobically).** One option is to use the **S.A.I.D.—Specific Adaptation to Intensity Demand principle** to overload the skill-technical movements related to the active muscles used in your sport participation to acquire optimum proficiency of the exercises representing the skill technique. **You should exercise at least as fast as the movements that your skill requires.**

2. SPEED PROGRAM.

(A) **Speed** is simply the product of stride length and stride frequency. Stride length is the distance that you cover with each step as you run.

(B) **Stride Frequency** is the number that you take per second. Your natural speed can be improved upon by the above.

(C) **Increasing**—i.e. **stride length.**

(D) **Increasing**—i.e. **stride frequency.**

3. SPEED POTENTIAL.

You cannot reach your full potential by simply running repetition sprints. A number of training elements must be fused together in order to achieve maximum speed potential.

TO DEVELOP PROPER SPRINTING-TECHNIQUES PROCEDURE: NINE ACCEPTED TECHNIQUES

Concentrate on the following points:

1. Drive off back leg—extending at ankle, knee and hips.
2. Swing heel up to hip.
3. Carry leg until the thigh is parallel to the ground.
4. Reach with the front leg forward.
5. Arms at a 90-degree angle, swinging independent of the shoulders—straight forward and backward.
6. On forward swing, make sure that the hands do not go above shoulder height.

SPRINT STARTING.

7. **Focus eyes on the ground about 20-30 yards ahead. The body-lean should be slightly forward.**
8. **Relax hands, arms, shoulders, neck and face. Fingers spread wide, thumbs up.**
9. **Breathe normally—do not hold your breath!**

Speed is often hindered by bio-mechanical (poor!) techniques for running. The correct technical form of a) stride length and b) stride frequency can be greatly enhanced by working on speed drills that include the correct technique. These drills assist you to develop a mechanically-efficient sprint form.

Improvement of stride length is accomplished by strength training specifically the legs, hips and thighs. Strength training, plyo-dynamics, flexibility and drills and also improved technique must be co-ordinated and combined with speed drills to develop maximum speed.

SPEED RUNNING: FIVE MAIN CHARACTERISTICS.

Running is characterised by:

1. **Higher knee-lift**—apex waist high.
2. **Increase in stride length—stride frequency.**
3. **Greater gyration of hips.**
4. **Greater drive of the arms.**
5. **Placement of the feet beneath the runner.**

CHARACTERISTICS DEFINED.

1. **The higher knee-lift** is to cover more ground forward or in front of the runner.
2. **The increase in stride** is to extend the stride length, during slow to medium speed—running (stride frequency).
3. **To increase the gyration of the hips** is to improve the frequency of the stride—overdrive of stride.
4. **Greater arm drive** facilitates the fluid and co-ordinated movement of arms and legs. The elbow drive must be accentuated—backwards rather than arms forwards, with fingers and thumbs extended—thumbs vertical. Front lift of the hands is restricted to the height of the shoulders—not above! Shoulders, flexibility and strength promote speed.

5. **The knee direction and ankle and toe placement**, with body placement just forward of the Centre of Gravityfacilitate placement of the feet under the body. For pure speed, knee and toe placement must be inwards to the body centre line. Pure power—knee and toe placement must be outwards. Breathe normally.

STRETCHING ROUTINE

AFTER WARM-UP USING CALISTHENICS

Flexibility exercises should be practised daily until the range of joint movement is optional through the full range of function. Kinesiological Principles related to Skill Analysis is to assess, analyse and determine, through practice and corrections sessions, any unnecessary **(A)**acceleration or **(B)**deceleration of movements in the vertical dimensions, i.e. accentuated high knee-lift and accentuated upward lift of the arms. The irregular movements should be eliminated and corrected bio-mechanically.

SPEED

Speed is the relative ability of the individual to move quickly and effectively and is dependent upon reaction, time, power and strength. This illustrates the integration of all fitness components. Speed appears to depend upon the ability of muscle fibres to contract and on the speed of impulse through the nerves supplying those particular fibres.

Speed is made up of two components—reaction time (the time the brain requires to recognise the signal and organise the requested movements) and movement time (the time required by the muscles to perform a movement following the signal from the brain.)

Power = Force (strength) !Velocity (speed).

This indicates very simply the relationship between power, strength and speed as a result increasing these components; Muscular Endurance should be improved.

POWER

A kinetic component.

Power is the capacity to exert maximum or near-maximum force of muscular contraction in any one effort to overcome resistance in the shortest possible time.

VARIOUS TRAINING MODES TO DEVELOP THE THREE ENERGY SYSTEMS.

% DEVELOPMENT.

TRAINING METHODS	A.T.P.P.C. & L.A.	L.A. & O2	OXYGEN (O_2)	ENERGY SYSTEMS
1. Acceleration Sprints.	90%	5%	5%	ANAEROBIC
2. Continuous Fast Running	2%	8%	90%	AEROBIC
3. Continuous Slow Running	2%	5%	93%	AEROBIC
4. Hollow Sprints	85%	10%	5%	ANAEROBIC
5. Interval Training	10 – 80%	10 – 80%	10 – 80%	SELECTED
5. Interval Sprinting	20%	10%	70%	AEROBIC
7. Jogging	–	–	100%	AEROBIC
8. Repetition Running	10%	50%	40%	ENDURANCE
9. Speed Play (Fartlek)	20%	40%	40%	INTERMIX SPEED-PLAY
10. Sprint Training	90%	6%	4%	ANAEROBIC

ABBREVIATIONS OF THE ENERGY SYSTEMS.

BIO-CHEMICAL ABBREVIATIONS:

(A.T.P) = ADENOSINE TRI-PHOSPHATE

(P.C) = PHOSPHO CREOTINE

(L.A) = LACTIC ACID

(O2) = OXYGEN

PRESCRIPTIONS FOR VARIOUS FIELD TRAINING METHODS

Nine training methods: Alternate days, alternate drills.

1. Acceleration Sprints: Anaerobic with technique.

Jog 50 to 120 yards, stride 50 to 120 yards, walk 50 to 120 yards, repeat.

2. Track or Field sprint training: Anaerobic with technique.

Spikes—running shoes. Repeat full speed sprints of 60 to 70 yards with active recovery between repeats.

3. Track or field hollow sprints: Aerobic with technique.

Spikes—running shoes. Sprint 60 yards, jog 60 yards, walk 60 yards, repeat until fatigued.

4. Track or field interval sprinting: Aerobic with technique.

Spikes—running shoes. Alternate 50-yard sprints with 60-yard jogs; repeat up to 3 miles.

5. Field training: Trainers. Speed play (fartlek)—Aerobic.

Jog 5 to 10 minutes, run ¾ to 1¼ miles at fast steady pace, walk 5 minutes, alternate jog sprint (65 to 75 yards) sprint uphill for 175 to 200 yards, jog for ¾ to 1¼ miles.

6. Field training: Trainers. Continuous fast running—Aerobic.

Run ¾ to 1¾ miles, steady fast pace (e.g. 6-minute mile pace), repeat 1 to 4 times. Run 8 to 10 miles, steady fast pace.

7. Field training: Trainers. Continuous slow running—Aerobic.

Run 6 to 12 miles steady slow pace (e.g. 7½-minute mile pace).

8. Field Training: Trainers. Jogging—Aerobic.

Jog 2 miles in 20 minutes.

9. Track or field interval training: Anaerobic sprints with technique. (Spikes—running shoes).

1 x 4 x 200 yds @ 30 secs. x 30 secs.—Recovery—Jogging.

2 x 8 x 100 yds @ 15 secs. x 30 secs.—Recovery—Walking.

It should be noted that these particular variations include movement patterns that are specifically involved in Rugby skills. It is thought that such training induces changes that are quite distinct from the training's effects on anaerobic metabolism.

The effects of training for high-power-output activities on anaerobic metabolism are not impressive, yet improvements in performance can be substantial. Obviously, some other changes induced by training must come into play. Possible factors that dictate performance changes in high-power-output activities are changes in motor unit recruitment patterns or chemical alterations at the neuro-muscular junction. Therefore, repeated performance of a specific motor skill or movement pattern involved in a high-power activity should contribute greatly to performance.

TO COMBINE SPEED AND ENDURANCE PRODUCES AEROBIC POWER, A LINE ENDURANCE WITH (2 x 6 MINUTES) MILES, BACK-TO-BACK EVERY TRAINING SESSION.

* To attain maximum effect from training and conditioning, use your age plus 85% of related Target Pulse Heart—Rate for at least 30 minutes, at the height of your program.
* Warm-up pre-training and conditioning.
* Stretch and limber all joints and muscles.
* Use the same warm-up routine to "cool down".

FIELD-DRILLS

SPEED & ENDURANCE DRILLS.
EACH PLAYER COMPLETE (4) 500 yds DRILL.
HALF SQUAD AT EACH END (2nd) 500 Yds.

START					FIELD
TOUCH EACH					25m
GRID					50m
LINE &					75m
RETURN					100m
					CONE
TIMED					MARKERS
					FINISH

400 yds × 9 = 3600yds)

(8) POWER AEROBIC ENDURANCE DRILLS.

SPRINT	CIRCUIT	ALTERNATE
STRAIGHTS	2 × 50yd Sprints	JOGS
BOUND	2 × 20yd Jogs	SPRINTS
BENDS	4 × Bounds	AND BOUNDS

(400yds)

(8) PLYO-DYNAMIC GRID DRILL (FREQUENCY).

1. LONG BOUNDS-USE ARMS.
2. SKIP BOUNDS-ALTERNATE FEET.
3. HOPS-ALTERNATE LEGS.
4. HIGH KNEE LIFT ALTERNATE LEGS.
5. HOP, SKIP AND BOUND (ALTERNATELY).
6. SPLIT JUMPS- ALTERNATE LEGS FORWARD.
7. DOUBLE (180') TWISTING JUMPS (LEFT& RIGHT).
8. STUTTER-SHORT TWIST JUMPS.

'THESE 3 DRILLS REPEAT IN ONE SESSION'.

FIELD PLYO-DYNAMIC DRILLS

CHAPTER 4D. P.M.A. POSITIVE MENTAL ATTITUDE IS THE BASIS OF PLYO-DYNAMIC TRAINING

Power: To understand the inner workings of the plyo-dynamic system and how they can be manipulated to create faster movements.

This chapter categorises various plyo-dynamic exercises and explains the effects that can be achieved by using them. Plyo-dynamic training can take many forms, including jump training for the lower extremities and strength exercises for the upper extremities. The user of plyo-dynamics should understand not only how to do the exercises, but also how to implement and modify a program and use it to its best advantage.

Jump-Training Exercises.

Early jump-training exercises were classified according to the relative demands they placed on the athlete. But all of them can be progressive in nature, with a low-to—high intensity in each type of exercise, plyo-dynamic "hops" and "jumps" on the basis of distance rather than type of exercise. Hops were exercises performed for distances less than 30 metres, while jumps were performed for distances greater than 30 metres. This classification can become confusing, the words "hop" and "jump" are used interchangeably.

Power can be thought of as the element which thrusts the entire body forward or in a direction suddenly and is concerned with pushing in scrums, tackling, running and kicking. A great amount of force is needed with each of the sudden exertions during these activities and as the development of power is closely related to strength and speed, any increase in power should bring an increase in velocity. Greater power is required when the load becomes heavier because power here becomes more dependent upon strength than speed. Consequently, it would appear that power would increase with increased strength.

1. Jumps—in—Place.

A jump-in-place is exactly that, a jump completed by landing in the same spot where the jump started. These exercises are relatively low intensity, yet they provide the stimulus for the athlete to rebound quickly from each jump. Jumps-in-place are done one after the other.

2. Standing Jumps.

A standing jump stresses single maximal effort, either horizontal or vertical. The exercise may be repeated several times, but full recovery should be allowed between each effort.

3. Multiple Hops and Jumps.

Multiple hops and jumps combine the skills developed by jumps-in-place and standing jumps; they require maximal effort but are done one after another. These exercises can be done alone or with a barrier. Multiple hops and jumps should be done for distances of less than 30 metres.

4. Bounding.

Bounding exercises exaggerate normal running stride to stress a specific aspect of the stride cycle. They are used to improve stride length and frequency. They typically are performed for distances greater than 30 metres.

5. Drills.

Jump drills combine multiple hops and jumps, they can be low in intensity or extremely stressful. They incorporate both horizontal and vertical components for successful completion.

FIELD DRILLS
POWER, SPEED & STRENGTH

Section 1. Power. A1.

A. Power is the combination of strength and speed. It refers to an athlete's ability to apply maximum force in the shortest period of time possible. It is essential in such sports as rugby—rucking and tackling, mauls, kicking and scrums and line-out jumping. Your power will increase as you increase your speed and/or strength.

B. Power can be greatly enhanced by simply doing the squat, hip sled or lunge. Your strength training should be supplemented by drills called plyo-dynamics. Plyo-dynamics cause your muscles to contract forcibly and quickly. (See D4).

PLANNING YOUR PROGRAM FOR POWER

Section 2. Speed. B2.

A. Speed is simply the product of stride length and stride frequency. Stride length is the distance that you cover with each step as you run. Stride frequency is the number of steps that you take per second. Your speed can be improved by increasing your stride length and/or stride frequency.

B. You cannot reach your full speed potential by simply running sprints. A number of training elements must be fused together in order to achieve maximum speed potential. Speed is often hindered by mechanically poor running form. Stride length and stride frequency can be greatly enhanced by working on the speed drills that improve technique. This helps you to develop a mechanically efficient sprint form.

C. Most experts on speed training tend to agree that concentrating your efforts on improving stride length attains the best results. Improvement of stride length is best accomplished by increasing the forces produced by the muscular contraction of the leg and hip muscles against the ground. Strength training and power drills in the next section enable you to contract your muscles more forcefully. Strength training, plyo-dynamics and flexibility drills to improve technique must be combined with running sprints into an effective program to develop maximum speed. Power sprints within your T.H.R. Aerobic Zone.

PLYO-DYNAMICS—COMBINED WITH SECTION 4

Section 3. Agility. C3.

A. Agility refers to an athlete's ability to change direction rapidly whilst maintaining balance without the loss of speed. An athlete must have good agility to be successful in sporting activities.

B. Your agility can be greatly enhanced by developing additional strength, speed and power but these components must be synchronised in a smooth, flowing motion. It would be wise to include agility drills when setting up your training program. The drills should incorporate forward, lateral and backward movements. They should also require you to change direction quickly while the body is in an awkward position. Three agility drills are provided here for your consideration; however, you should test, evaluate and set goals before concentrating on your program. Attention—Interchange the Program with Power Aerobics.

COMBINE PLYO-DYNAMICS WITH AGILITY DRILLS

Section 4. Procedure. D4.

A. **Drill 1** 10/10 Hopping. With 10-yard lateral sprints and inter-spacing. Starting on the right leg, hop as fast as possible for ten yards. Switch immediately to the left leg and hop another ten yards. Alternate from right to left for a total of forty to sixty yards. Emphasise hopping as fast as possible. Combine with Agility Drills.

B. **Drill 2**. Power Hopping. On one leg, hop for as much distance as possible for three to seven hops. Repeat using the other leg. Lateral sprint after each set for 10 yards, continue for 40 to 60 yards.

C. **Drill 3.** Power Jumping on single leg. Jump as far as possible for three to seven jumps. Sprint 10 yards and change directions.

D. **Drill 4.** Speed Jumping on Single leg. Jump as fast as possible for distance of twenty to forty yards. Sprint 20 yards. Angle Sprints.

E. **Drill 5.** Single leg hop—5 on Left leg and 5 on right leg. Value to develop explosiveness for starting power and acceleration. Sprint 10 yards after each set.

MODERN SCIENTIFIC TRAINING

Circuit Training • 2. Interval Training • 3. Integrating Aerobic Training • 4. Alternate Muscle Function Training.

Four Circuit Training Systems: (1. C.T.) (2. I.T.) (3. I.A.T.) (4. M.F.T.)

Circuit training has well-defined and limited aims. It is not designed to supplant weight training for the weight lifter or endurance running for the long-distance runner, though both of these types of athlete could use it with advantage. It is a form of general fitness training based on sound physiological principles and aiming at the kind of varied activity and continuous challenge which are attractive to large numbers of young men, many of whom show little enthusiasm for ordinary forms of physical training.

Many forms of circuit training can be devised to meet specific needs and apparatus would be used in many cases. The type of circuit training described in this manual is suggested because it was necessary to devise a circuit which coaches could use in conjunction with other forms of training, without having to set up special equipment.

Circuit training can involve a deal of strengthening exercises with weights. These are omitted from the Rugby Mod circuit, the emphasis is on physical exercise, coupled with running to promote agility, endurance and speed with staying power. Thus, the only equipment a coach needs is a stopwatch and markers to show the position, type and number of repetitions of the exercise to be performed at a particular point.

1. Callisthenics.—2. Dumb-Bells.—3. Plyo-dynamics—4. Progressive Bar—Bell

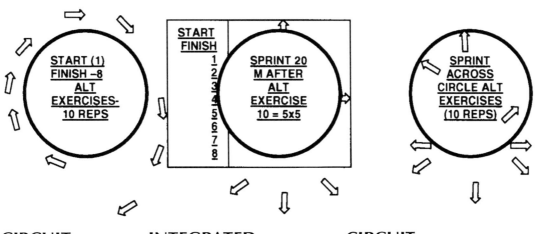

CIRCUIT	INTEGRATED	CIRCUIT
Warm up	Power Exercises	Resistance Exercises
Use Cones	Use Cones	Bar-Bells
10 reps	Sprint 20-m outward	Sprint across Circle
Sprint Circuit		and back to next cone

Rugby mod circuit training is essentially a hard, continuous bout of strenuous exercise wherein selected exercises are performed a specified number of times depending on the player's requirements.

Plyo-dynamic drills to facilitate spatial awareness

    A. **Attention span**—improvement.

    B. **Awareness span**—extension.

    C. **Kinaesthetics.**

    D. **Awareness.**

Exercise Drills to facilitate A, B, C & D.

1. **Skip jumps.** Alternate legs (continuous)—three single steps in-between each skip jump.
2. **Alternate leg bounding.** Three single bound steps in-between each bound.
3. **Single-leg speed hops.** With (A) knee tucks and heel to buttocks (B)—fling both arms as high as possible.
4. **Double-leg speed jumps.** Three steps in between each knee tuck—(A) right leg lead and (B) left leg lead.
5. **Double-leg long jumps.** Three small steps in between each bound.
6. **Alternate leg hops.** A hop-step-jump sequence with left (3 bounds) right (alternate).
7. **Four plyo-kinetic drills**—A, B, C & D.

THE MODERN PLYO-DYNAMICS

6 Phase Hexagon Drills.

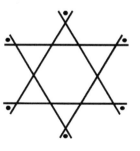

1. **Monday** - One full circuit – 20 yd sprint, standard jumps, 5 × circuits × 5 × sprints. Variations in directions.
2. **Tuesday** – Half twists – 5-25 yd sprints to clockwise.
3. **Wednesday** – Half twists – 5-30 yds sprints clockwise.
4. **Thursday** – Sideways jumps – 5 × 35 yd sprints (3 & 5) anti clockwise (2 & 5) clockwise.

Each drill contains one complete circuit jumps two foot with 5 different sprint distances (20-35 yards). Use cones or hurdles.

Explosive plyo-dynamic and agility drills interacting five different techniques with five different sprint distances and directions.

INTERVAL TRAINING
POWER COURSE, POWER AEROBICS

COURSE DISTANCES - 25 x 2, 30 x 2, 35 x 2, 40 x 2, 50 x 2
50m 60m 70m 80m 100m

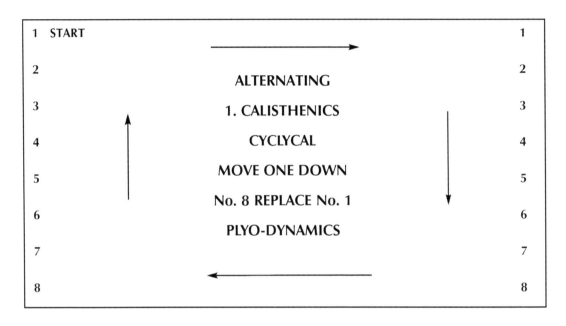

INTERVAL = ALTERNATE, CYCLICAL AND CIRCUIT TRAINING

COMPLETE CIRCLE SPRINT AFTER EACH EXERCISE
CIRCUIT POWER AEROBICS

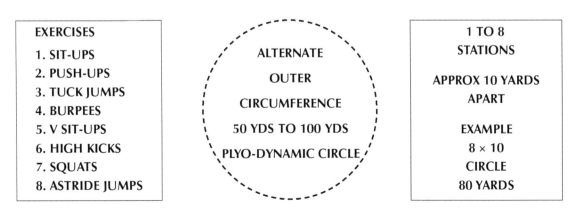

COMBINE WITH PLYO-DYNAMICS

SECTION 4

FITNESS AND TRAINING

SPORT PARTICIPATION

TECHNIQUES AND WEIGHT TRAINING EXERCISE PROGRAMME

HEALTH AND FITNESS

BY BERT HOLCROFT

FOUR SYSTEM TRAINING ANALYSIS.

Referring to

(1) Circuit of differing exercises with weights to cover the full musculature function of every joint in the body, not only the protagonist muscles but the antagonist as well. The protagonist muscle is obviously developed by the concentric system of function but the antagonist muscle is developed by the eccentric system of function—that is, the muscle contracts whilst lengthening, i.e. lowering the weights slowly to their starting position gives an eccentric action function, simplified and applied.

(2) Interval Training.

Like circuit training is self explanatory, so is interval training. You rest during and after each set of exercises. During exercise, you rest in-between each exercise. For example: The amount of time after each session of set of reps, you do callisthenics for 2-3 minutes to reduce the amount of lactic acid build-up by the break-down of the muscle fibres during contraction and function of muscles, using the overload principle and method. Each of the Methods of Overload employed in Interval Training consists of a series of method and expected outcome until the entire muscular structure has been exercised at least three times. This is possible for the stress-related action is very low and gives the muscle plenty of recovery time. Do these exercises without resting in-between sets, otherwise you defeat the purpose. A sequence of 3 exercises suggested could be: (a) squats, (b) dumb-bell presses or (c) abdominals. Each sport and each participant has different requirements; therefore each sports participant should select a programme and training method suitable to his choice of sport and goal achievement.

(3) Integrated Aerobic Training is a recent concept of endurance training. It is similar to Fartlek Training but designed to adapt weight training, ie. Progressive Resistant Overload Principle, instead of terrain obstacle course of the Fartlek era. This is obtained by designing a mixture of circuit and active interval training over a measured area, (a) large indoor hall, (b) gymnasium or (c) a small portion of a field marked with cones or flags to dictate the course of direction. The object is to select a number of exercises for weight training specifically for the upper body and neck and rely on a relay of runs designed to activate (a) the cardio-vascular system and (b) the lower part of the anatomy from the waist down. Lay the flags on both sides of the designated arena. Start with the weights. When you have completed the designated activity of exercise across and back to the next flag and set of weights, continue this exercise for at least:

   (A) 8 x progressive overload exercises combined with
   (B) 8 x activities across the arena.

Monitor your heart rate during the execution of these exercises.

(4) A.M.F. Alternate Muscle Function Training.

This type of scientific training is to use the overload principle of training that will reduce body fat and improve cardio-vascular facilitation. The basic theory of A.M.F. is by altering one's basic metabolic rate. The body would have to cope with more calories and thus convert the stored fat into energy. To use the A.M.F. system correctly, one has to determine a set routine of exercises that are far removed from the norm. The general idea is to work one set of muscles and then select an exercise that works a set of muscle far removed from the first. This arrangement of exercises is designed to do a number of things. First, the heart is required to work constantly moving blood to areas of the body that are at extreme position-wise in the muscular structure.

The Four systems covered have the capacity to deliver relatively high levels of strength, local muscle endurance and cardio-respiratory endurance, i.e. aerobic capacity is determined by personal endeavour and goal. These four systems of cyclic training should be combined with speed training, flexibility, agility, power and skill training to maximise conditional facilitation of selected sporting participation.

ATTAINING ELITE STANDARDS

1. Circuit. 2. Interval. 3. I.A.T and 4. A.M.F. training defined.

(1) Circuit Training is self-explanatory. Of these four components combined, this has the capacity to deliver relatively high levels of cardio-respiratory endurance, local muscular endurance, agility and strength. These four non-scientific systems of Cyclical Interval Training, should be associated with:
Speed Training.

1. Flexibility
2. Agility Grids
3. Power Grids—plyo-dynamics
4. Skill Training—circuit A.M.F.—A.T.

Combine with interval training relating to an active exercise in between each specific group of exercises. To define and explain and to simplify the above:

(1)Circuit training refers to a circuit of any dimensions or design, i.e. circle, square, oblong, zig-zag, etc., with correct intensity exercises to cover every joint and muscle group in the body. All of these mod groups of exercises utilise the **(2) Interval Training Method**, that is, after each group of exercises, a new form of movements is introduced, continuous callisthenics and all forms of running—sprinting, jogging, striding, jumping, hopping etc, to alleviate and reduce the amount of muscular lactic acid build up during the resistance period of exercise. Build up is by breaking down function of muscles being exercised by the overload principle. Bar-bells or dumb—bells.

(3) Integrating Training relates to Endurance Aerobic Capacity, combining Circuit and Interval Training, i.e. 3-mile circuit and using the full length of the football field of approximately 5000 metres, timed sets with intervals combining resistance type of exercises with 400, 600 and 800 metres. Fartlek interval-type training is designed to combine Circuit, Interval and I.A.T.

(4) Alternating Muscle Function training is a modern concept of scientific principle to improve the Cardio-Respiratory Vascular System by altering one's basic metabolism. This type of training reduces body fat, as well as improving the energy System. This new mod concept of exercises differs from the norm! The general idea is to design a format which determines a set routine of drills working complete opposite groups of muscles within the circuit or interval system, i.e. to use progressive resistance exercises by weights (dumb-bells and bar-bells). You would arrange your circuit so that No. 1 would be upper body, No.2 would be lower body. These alternate and continue through your full circuit. This format puts your heart under constant stress, pumping blood from upper body to lower body, alternately and consistently, thus developing the areas of the body distal to the heart.

AFTER-STRETCHING ROUTINE: TEST FOR FITNESS LEVELS

OXYGEN UPTAKE CAPACITY TESTS (15 MINS TEST)
CHART OF AEROBIC FITNESS

This test is similar to the 15-mile aerobic fitness run except that here you can fairly accurately predict your maximum oxygen uptake capacity. Take the test on a 440-yard running track or on a level course of known length. Have a friend time the run for you, he can also count laps, indicate the time remaining and mark your position at the end of 15 minutes.

Scoring: Run at a pace you can maintain for a full 15 minutes. Figure the total distance covered (e.g. 8¼ laps of 440 yards). Convert to yards and divide by 15 to get the average running speed per minute. Then simply use Fig. 2 and table 1 to figure your cardio-respiratory fitness level.

$$8¼ \times 440 \text{yds} = 3630 / 15 == 242 \text{ yds / minute.}$$

$$242 \text{yds/min} = 48 \text{ml / kg / min. (MAX VO2).}$$

PHYSICAL EXERCISE—SEE EXERCISE CHARTS

(1) Front Upper Arm—(Biceps).

Combined with chest muscles are important for pushing, pulling and running. Promotes strength and power.

TWO ARM CURL

UPPER BODY

(2) Shoulder—(Deltoid).

Important for lifting, pulling, throwing and gripping. This muscle, when well-developed, assists in preventing shoulder injuries.

PRESS BEHIND NECK

(3) Neck & Upper Back. (TRAPEZIUS)

These muscles are important to keep the shoulders back. If they fall forward because of over-developed Pectorals, the lung capacity may be limited.

UPPER BODY

(4) Front Thigh—(Quadraceps).

The important muscles of the leg necessary for driving power in running and strengthening of these muscles should assist in the prevention of most knee injuries.

PROGRESSIVE RESISTANCE EXERCISES
(SEE EXERCISE CHARTS)

(5) Calf—(Gastrocnemius).

This is an important driving muscle extending to the Achilles tendon in the lower legand gives the foot a strong muscle.

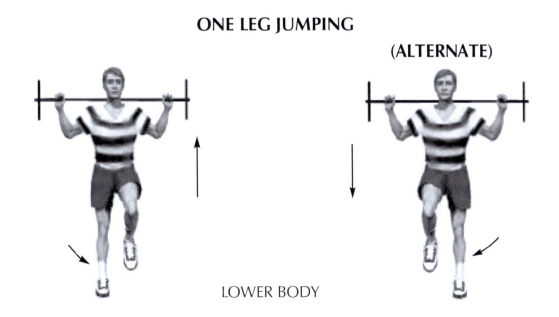

(6) Inside Thigh—(Vastus Internus).

This muscle is really in the same class as chart No.15 but the problems tend to arise more in the groin region.

UP & DOWN, DOUBLE JUMP – SIDEWAYS & FORWARDS STRADDLE HOPS

Buttocks – (Gluteals).

The main driving muscles of the legs. They are very important in running.

LOWER BODY.

(7) Lower Back—(Erector Spinal).

These muscles are responsible for keeping the discs solidly intact and are important in bending, pushing and lifting movements. They are an important set of muscles for good posture.

THE BEND-OVER (SLOWLY)

MID & LOWER BODY.

8. Code of Muscles. Shoulder Deltoids (See Exercise Charts).

Important for lifting, pulling, throwing and gripping. This muscle when well-developed assists in preventing shoulder injuries.

Important for lifting, holding or pulling. This muscle also assists in holding the collarbone to prevent a break.

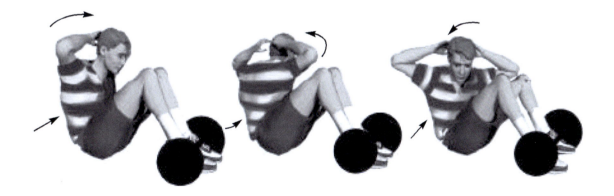

(9) Front Stomach—(Abdominals).

These are important to endurance since they assist with the return of blood from the legs and therefore must possess strength and muscular endurance. These muscles also protect against internal injuries.

ALTERNATE POWER AEROBICS

COURSE DISTANCES - 25 x 2, 30 x 2, 35 x 2, 40 x 2, 50 x 2.

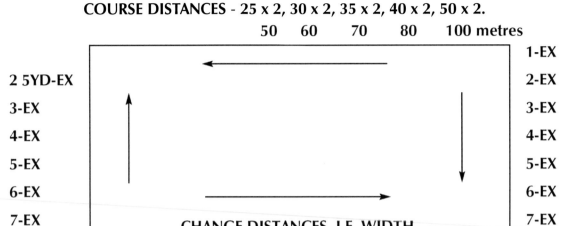

PROGRESSIVE RESISTANCE GRIDS
BAR BELLS EXERCISE. 2. DUMB-BELLS & EXERCISES.

	75 lbs.15 REPS			15lb × DUMB-BELLS	AEROBICS
1	OVERHEAD PRESS	SPRINT	1	ALT BICEP CURLS	AS
2	HALF SQUATS	ZIG ZAG	2	SIDEWAY FLYS	AS
3	ARM CURLS	SKIP STEP	3	ALT D-BELL PRESS	AS
4	CLEAN & PRESS	LEFT FOOT HOP	4	ALT SIDE BEND	AS
5	UP RIGHT ROW	RIGHT FOOT HOP	5	ALT TRICEP STRETCH	AS
6	FULL SQUAT	BOUNDING	6	BEND OVER FLYS	AS
7	BENT OVER ROW	L/R SHORT STEP	7	ALT FORWARD RAISE	AS
8	SPLIT JUMPS	RUN FORWARD	8	OVERHEAD S/ARM RAISE	AS
	EVERY 10M YDS TURN	BACKWARD		STRAIGHT ARMS	AS

AEROBICS AND EXERCISES 1+2 CONTINUOUS.
USE FLAGS AS MARKERS (5 METRES APART).
AGILITY DRILLS USING CONES.
***SEE PERCENTAGE SOMATOGRAPH WEIGHTS CHART.**

BIO-MECHANICS & PHYSIOLOGY

PERSONAL AWARENESS & APPLICATION
(SEE PAGE 63), (CHART I)—UPPER BODY

(1) Chest—(Pectorals).
These big muscles are necessary for pushing and pulling and their development is important for strength and power.

(2) Front upper arm—(Biceps).
Combined with chest muscles are important for pushing, pulling and running.

(3) Forearm—(Flexors and Extensors).
These are important in throwing, catching and gripping or any activity requiring the use of the forearms.

(4) Upper back and neck—(Trapezius).
Important for lifting, holding or pulling.

(5) Shoulder—(Deltoid).
Important for lifting, pulling, throwing and gripping.

(6) Front stomach—(Abdominals).
These are important to endurance since they assist with the return of blood from the legs and therefore must possess strength and muscular endurance.

(7) Side stomach—(External Obliques).
These protect against internal injuries.

(8) Rear upper arm—(Triceps)
Assists with Biceps group.

(9) Side chest—(Serratus Magnus).
These muscle, along with the inter-costals between the ribs, lift the chest and play an important part in assisting the expansion of the lungs to get a maximum intake of oxygen per breath.

PHYSIOLOGY PROFICIENCIES

PRINCIPLES & APPLICATIONS
(SEE PAGE CHART II)

(10) Neck and upper back—(Rhomboids)
These muscles are important to keep the shoulders back.

LOWER BODY

(11) Lower back—(Erector Spinal).
These muscles are responsible for keeping the discs solidly intact and are important in bending, pushing and lifting movements.

(12) Front thigh—(Quadraceps).
The important muscles of the leg necessary for driving power in running.

(13) Broad back—(Latissimus Dorsi).
This is important in pulling, lifting and throwing.

(14) Buttox—(Gluteals).
The main driving muscles of the legs. This is very important in running.

(15) Rear thigh (Biceps Femoris).
Driving muscles of the leg. Commonly known as Hamstring muscles.

(16) Inside thigh (Vastus Internus).

(17) Outside thigh (Vastus Extermus).
These muscles are in the same class as No. 15 but the problems tend to arise more in the groin region.

(18) Calf (Gastrocemius).
This is an important driving muscle extending to the Achilles tendon in the lower leg and gives the foot a strong thrust.

ALTERNATE MUSCLE GROUPS TO ACHIEVE FUNCTIONAL MAXIMUM HEART ACTION.

REACHING A PEAK

BIO-MECHANICS & PHYSIOLOGY: MODERN SCIENTIFIC DISCIPLINES

(A) Anterior View.

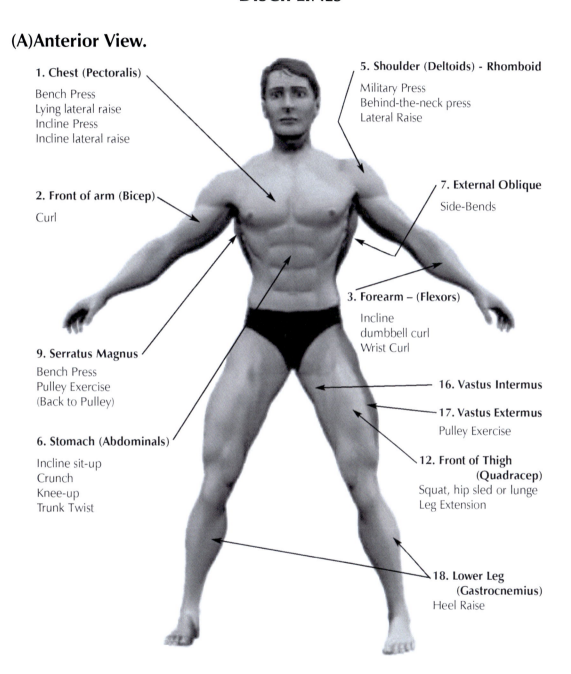

1. Chest (Pectoralis)
   Bench Press
   Lying lateral raise
   Incline Press
   Incline lateral raise

5. Shoulder (Deltoids) - Rhomboid
   Military Press
   Behind-the-neck press
   Lateral Raise

2. Front of arm (Bicep)
   Curl

7. External Oblique
   Side-Bends

3. Forearm – (Flexors)
   Incline dumbbell curl
   Wrist Curl

9. Serratus Magnus
   Bench Press
   Pulley Exercise
   (Back to Pulley)

16. Vastus Intermus

17. Vastus Extermus
    Pulley Exercise

6. Stomach (Abdominals)
   Incline sit-up
   Crunch
   Knee-up
   Trunk Twist

12. Front of Thigh
    (Quadracep)
    Squat, hip sled or lunge
    Leg Extension

18. Lower Leg
    (Gastrocnemius)
    Heel Raise

ANATOMY CHART—(FRONT)
USE WEIGHT APPLICATOR (PAGE)

TERMS AND DEFINITIONS.
SPORT PARTICIPATION.

BIO-MECHANICS & PHYSIOLOGY: TERMS & DEFINITIONS
RELEVANT TERMS AND THEIR MEANING

(B) Posterior View.

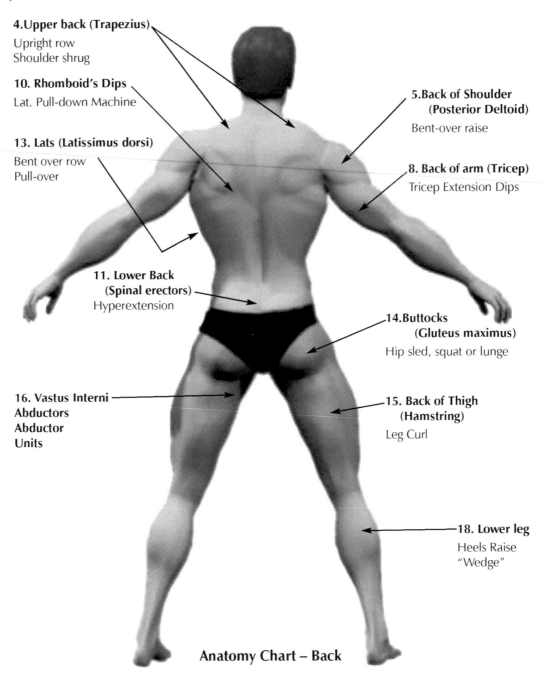

Anatomy Chart – Back

FOR (18) USE WEDGE UNDER FEET WIDTH AT LEAST (2" x 5cm) UTILISE WEIGHT-ASSESSMENT CHART (PAGE 65).

STARTING PROGRESSIVE WEIGHTS RESISTANCE SOMATOGRAPH PERCENTAGES

CODE OF MUSCLES	REPS	BODY % WEIGHTS
1. CHEST (PECTORALS)	2 × 5	BODY WEIGHT
2. FRONT UPPER ARM (BICEPS)	2 × 10	(FREE WEIGHTS) 25% BODY WEIGHT
3. FOREARM (FLEXORS & EXTENSIONS)	2 × 10	(FREE WEIGHTS) 25% BODY WEIGHT
4. UPPER BACK & NECK (TRAPIS)	2 × 5	(FREE WEIGHTS) 30% BODY WEIGHT
5. SHOULDER (DELTOIDS)	2 × 10	(FREE WEIGHTS) 30% BODY WEIGHT
6. FRONT STOMACH (ABDOMINALS)	2 × 5	(SIT UP UNIT) 10% BODY WEIGHT
7. SIDE OF STOMACH (EXTERNAL)	2 × 5	(PULLEY MACHINE) 10% BODY WEIGHT
8. REAR UPPER ARM (TRICEPS)	1 × 10	(FREE WEIGHTS) 15% BODY WEIGHT

1. CIRCUIT POWER COURSE GRAPH.

2. PROGRESSIVE RESISTANCE GRID CHART.

3. MUSCLE FUNCTION ACTION CIRCUIT.

4. INTERVAL POWER COURSE CHART.

2. SOMATOGRAPH SETS AND % WEIGHT

CODE OF MUSCLES	REPS	BODY % WEIGHTS
9. SIDE OF CHEST (SERRATUS MAGIMUS)	2 × 5	(PULLEY MACHINE) 10% BODY WEIGHT
10. UPPER BACK (RHOMBOIDS)	2 × 5	(FREE WEIGHTS) BODY WEIGHT
11. LOWER BACK (ERECTOR SPINAE)	2 × 5	(FREE WEIGHTS) 2BODY WEIGHT
12. FRONT OF THIGH (QUADRACEPS)	2 × 5	(MULTI EXERCISER) 30% BODY WEIGHT
13. BROAD OF BACK (LATISSIMUS DORSI)	2 × 5	(MULTI EXERCISER) 30% BODY WEIGHT
14. BUTTOCKS (GLUTEALS)	2 × 5	(SQUAT FREE WEIGHTS) BODY WEIGHT
15. REAR OF THIGHS (BICEPS FERIMOUS)	2 × 5	(MULTI EXERCISER) 30% BODY WEIGHT
16. INSIDE OF THIGHS (VASTUS INTERNUS)	2 × 5	(ABDUCTOR UNITS) ADJUSTMENT
17. OUTSIDE THIGHS (VASTUS EXTERNUS)	2 × 5	(ABDUCTOR UNIT)
18. CALF MUSCLE (GASTROCEMIUS))	2 × 5	30% BODY WEIGHT
19. LOWER FOOT (PLANTAR GROUPS)	2 × 5	AS ABOVE

1. PROGRESSIVELY INCREASE (NUMBER OF SETS).

2. INCREASE GRID AND CIRCUIT WIDTH AND CIRCUMFERENCE.

3. MONITOR % OF BODY WEIGHT PROGRESSIVELY.

ALTERNATE MUSCLE FUNCTION ACTION CIRCUITS

CIRCUIT—POWER AEROBICS

5 ¥ DISTANCE
DISTANCES
1 = CIRCLE (50 YDS)
2 = CIRCLE (60 YDS)
3 = CIRCLE (70 YDS)
4 = CIRCLE (80 YDS)
5 = CIRCLE (100 YDS)

OUTER CIRCUMFERENCE
50 YDS – 100 YDS

1 – 8
STATIONS
APPROX 10 YDS APART
EXAMPLE:
  8 x 10 CIRCLE
  80 YDS
  15 x REPS EACH

SEE PERCENTAGE WEIGHTS CHART

DUMB BELLS **BAR BELLS**

CONTINUOUS = PROGRESSIVE	RESISTANCE EXERCISES, SPRINTS
1. = DUMB-BELL CURL = SPRINT FULL CIRCLE	1. = BICEP CURL = FULL CIRCLE
2. = FORWARD D/B RAISE ALT	2. = BENT-OVER ROW = FULL CIRCLE
3. = BENT-OVER D/B LATERAL RAISE	3. = SINGLE-FOOT LUNGE, ALT
4. = SIDE LATERAL D/B RAISE	4. = HALF SQUAT, ALT
5. = SINGLE TRICEP STRETCH	5. = UP RIGHT ROW
6. = SINGLE D/B PRESS, ALT	6. = CLEAN & PRESS
7. = ALT SIDE BENDS	7. = PRESS OVER HEAD (HIGH)
8. ALT STRAIGHT ARM RAISE	8. = CLEAN & JERK & SPLIT & PRESS
SPRINT AS FAST AS POSSIBLE	BREATHE NORMAL CONTINUOUS

**EACH STATION = 15 REPS 1 TO 8.
SPRINT ONE FULL CIRCLE IN BETWEEN EACH SET OF REPS.
PROCEED TO EACH STATION EXERCISE AFTER EACH FULL CIRCLE SPRINT.
CIRCUIT CONTINUOUS 1-8 STATION.**

REF: SOMATOGRAPH PERCENTAGE WEIGHTS CHART

TARGET HEART RELATED PROGRAM

PERSONAL COMMITMENT PROGRAM
MONDAY, WEDNESDAY AND FRIDAY

Before this part of the programme is attempted, you should have built up a base of aerobic fitness.

6 minutes—1 mile

2 miles x 12 minutes (back to back)

Power aerobic fitness, 3 miles x 18 minutes (target).

Repetition Hill Work: Concentrics.

For one run a week, go out for a five-to-ten-minutes' warm-up jog until you have come to the hill you have decided to run up. Start at half pace and build up to three-quarter pace running with correct technique until you find you cannot hold form any longer. The distance you run depends upon the gradient of hill but between 40 metres for a steep gradient to around 70 metres for a lesser gradient. Turn around and jog back down to the start of the flat before repeating five more times. Slowly build up to ten repetitions for strength and stamina. Eccentrics—reverse the above drill—sprint down the hill and jog.

Please note: The repetition hill-work should be attempted just after warm-ups when you are working more intensely on your aerobic fitness and not immediately pre—season, when you will be running on the flat surface that you are going to play on! Do not run on roads, concrete or any surface too solid (causes Muscle Injury and Shin Splints.

Agilities.

For a change in your anaerobic training, you may like to practice agility running—whether it is shuttle runs, running backwards and dodging or weaving around markers—-this type of running is very applicable to the game. Let your imagination be the limiting factor in the types of agilities you choose. Repeat them in sets of five and do a good twenty-to-thirty-minute workout (including warm-up and cool-down jogs and a few basic stretches.).

PHILOSOPHY OF TRAINING
Modern training for Elitism in Sport

With correct attitude, sacrifice and regular training: **(A)** Your body systems adapt to absorb more pressure and tension. **(B)** As your training increases in intensity, temperament and perseverance are very important. **(C)** You have to accept the philosophy of Scientific—-Gradual Physical Adaptation in the Nine Levels of Fitness.

SECTION 5

COACHING KNOWLEDGE

FOOTBALL SCIENTIFIC ANALYSIS

Accreditation

PSYCHOLOGICAL & PHYSIOLOGICAL FACTORS, INTERACTING, INTERCHANGING, INTEGRATING, TO ATTAIN NEW PHILOSOPHIES FOR SUPREMACY.

UPGRADED ILLUSTRATIONS AND TECHNIQUES THROUGH MODERN SCIENTIFIC PRINCIPLES.

FACILITATING A NEW MODE OF TECHNICAL PROFICIENCIES FOR SOCCER

SOCCER PARTICIPANTS

BERT HOLCROFT (FITNESS FOR SPORT GURU)

INTRODUCING FUTURISTIC SCIENCES IN SPORT PARTICIPATION

—CYBERVISION AND PSYCHO-CYBERNETICS
M.I.T.—MENTAL IMAGERY PERCEPTION
M.I.P—SKILL MEMORY PROGRAMMING
M.I.R.—ENGRAMS SYNTHESIS PROCEDURE

"VISUAL AND VIDEO PERCEPTION" BY "VIDEO ANALYSTS"

THE **"FUTURISTIC"** METHOD OF TEACHING **(SKILL TECHNIQUES AND PROFICIENCIES)**, REFERS TO **(VIDEO ANALYSIS SYNTHESIS)**. AN **"EXPERT"** IN THE **"SPORT INVOLVED"**, DETERMINES THE **"PERFECTLY PERFORMED SKILL"** AND SPECIFYS THE MOVEMENT TO THE **"PARTICIPANT"**, WHO, IN TURN VIEWS THE **"SKILL"** TO ESTABLISH A **"MENTAL IMAGERY MOVEMENT"**, FOR FUTURE RE-ENACTMENT OF THATSKILL,**(M.I.P), (M.I.T.) AND (M.I.R.) (MENTAL IMAGE PROGRAMMING), (MENTAL IMAGE TRAINING) AND (MENTAL IMAGE REHEARSAL) "FACILITATING"**

"MENTAL IMAGERY PERCEPTION"
THROUGH
"CYBERVISION AND PSYCHO-CYBERNETICS"

IN PLAIN "TERMS", GET AN EXPERT TO STUDY ALL THE GAMES THE PLAYERS HAVE PARTICIPATED IN WITH A GREAT PERSONAL SATISFACTION, SELECT THEIR MOST PRESTIGIOUS MOMENTS AND **"ON VIDEOS"** i.e. **(A VIDEO ANALYST)**.

"ENGRAM SYNTHESIS PROCEDURE" BY (VIDEO LOOPS)

SELECT THE **CLIPS**WHERE **"HE" OR "SHE"**, HAS **DONE SOMETHING WELL** AND PUT THEM ALL ON "ONE VIDEO" AND GET THEM TO VIEW IT REPEATEDLY TO FACILITATE **"AUTOMONOUS REFLEX ACTION, OF THOSE ACCREDITED SKILLS.**

"Analysis of the (A x B x C x D & E) of the Physiology of Soccer"

Analysis and diagnosis of physiological requirements, conducted during a "Fitness and Proficiencies Training Program:

(a) **Defining the contents of the session,**

(b) **Allowing the coach or players to interpret and design individual training and conditioning programs;**

(c) **Profiling strengths and weaknesses, defining and specifying "Bio-Mechanics" of movements and techniques,**

(d) **Correcting previous technical deficiencies,**

(e) **Developing new modified drills creating new formats, culminating in designing and defining more efficient and proficiencies technical skills.**

It is not advisable for soccer players to concentrate **all his emphasis,** on just the technical aspects such as i.e. **(Ball control in close play)**, **(dribbling)**, **(passing)**, **(kicking, i.e. cross-overs)**, **(shots at goal)** etc., if he does not have the necessary **"fitness and conditioning"** to carry out these newly **acquired skill techniques, to facilitate a successful contribution during the (90 minutes) of competitive play.** Remember **"Defensive Qualities"** are just as important as **"Attacking Skills",** to culminate a **successful conclusion. If the players do not have accredited Somatograph of fitness levels, they would fail in their endeavour to achieve acceptable standards of technical proficiencies of excellence".** In soccer there are **(10) ten,** field positions and one specialist position i.e. **(Goal Keeper).** All of these positions vary in stature and structure, requiring different applications of skill techniques and attributes, it is therefore advisable and desirable to attain your **"Ultimate Levels of Fitness".** To achieve this goal, you must assess and analyse every aspect of **your selected positional requirements, proportional strengths and weaknesses, to allow you to facilitate your (Game Plan), (Tactics) and (Strategies), formulated for your individual skill to be combined into a powerful accomplished and successful unit.** The coach should identify his charges particular talents and the position suitable to achieve co-ordination of all individual expertise into a successful format, by **defining, determining, and implementing these individualistic characteristics and idiosyncrasies into tactical and strategical game plans.** The co-ordinating of all these facets of play should be tested under game pressure conditions i.e. **(full scale practice)** also **(one on one) practice for skills** which should involve confrontations such as **"contact impact collision"** game situations, and by observation to determine meaningful concept of achievement. It **is an accepted scientific fact that constant repetitive drills of the "correct technical skills" you wish to acquire, will replicate themselves unobtrusively into your autonomous reflex system,** correcting and replacing those previous **(Bad Habits)**thus creating a far more efficient and proficient response, in your endeavour to improve implementation and facilitation of your newly acquired soccer skills. (Previous **Bad Habits having been scientifically replaced with Good Habits.**) By attaining, retaining and promoting these new skills, you instigate a greater influence on the result of the game. There is one very important aspect of your performance, and that relates to your **"fitness levels"**. If your fitness levels do not attain the **(48 pts—Somatograph chart levels**you can rest assured that your skill levels or **(lack of)**, will reflect your performance levels, it is nigh impossible to promote your new found technical proficiencies, if your fitness levels **do not reach, i.e. (58.2—V˙O2, MAX-48 pts equated)** of your **"Somatograph.** A scientific clinical proven fact is, that your **autonomous system will be ineffective,** therefore **reducing your** skill output levels.

"PROFESSIONAL"

"Soccer Illustrations and Demonstrations"

Demonstration and practice, after adaption of these modernised techniques and skills, will convert players individual personal contribution into a **"Professional modem of skilled proficiencies.** These modern fitness levels allow the implementation of techniques, **promoting players skill levels** beyond their wildest dreams, converting their endeavour from an also ran into a champion, upto International levels of achievements. To "**BE A WINNER**" you must be aware of and accept that **skill**, unlike **fitness,**is a consequence of practicing the **correct technical proficiencies** repetitively, specifically your newly acquired technical proficiencies. To achieve these levels and goals, requires hours of dedicated and repetitive practice of the correct movements, relating to the techniques, and drills, in your ultimate endeavour to **eradicate former incorrect techniques, (which have previously cultivated, "Bad Habits" producing inadequate and unacceptable, "Unforced Error Situations").** To correct these inadequacies you must apply the **"Three Phases"** of accepted principles of learning, to achieve these desirable attributes of:

(**a**) Cognitive

(**b**) Associative, and

(**c**) Autonomy

"Applications and Principles"

(a) **"Cognitive"** equates with **(the knowledge of)**

(b) **"Association"** equates with **(combining and associations)**

(c) **"Autonomy"** equates with **(automotive reflexes)**

There is an accepted analysis, that without these **(3) phases,** sequential skills acquisition is not attainable. To differentiate from **"SKILL AND HABIT"**, **"Skill"** just like **Habit** is acquired, but a crucial and meaningful difference exists, separating the two; a **"Skill"** is performed, a **"Habit"** is exercised. There are i.e. **(Good Habits)** and **(Bad Habits).** The comparative difference between these two expletives is that **"Skill"**, is adaptable and flexible, **"Habits"** once formed are **adapted**! The **"Habits"** we are referring to in this chapter are **"Bad Habits"**! Unfortunately these functions become repetitive, especially under stressful and pressure situations. It is an acceptable fact that these anomalies can be converted into something special. Repetition of your previous acquired skill-drills can advance you into the field of expertise, by erasing all your previous **"Bad Habits"** and replacing them with advanced **"Skill techniques"** i.e. **(Good Habits)** of a very high standard. To facilitate these technical proficient skills, involves the player's ability to co-ordinate and implement corrections under difficult circumstances, the **player or coach initiates** the appropriate feed back to **(defuse)** or **(continue)** an ongoing situation.

Philosophies of the Soccer Elite

(a) Activating the required interpretation promoted by internal and external clues, observations and adaptability,

(b) **(The autonomous adopted reflexes, relate to a quicker and more exact proficient reaction to the appropriate requirements.)**

(c) Reduces the reaction time of identification of your selected responses to deal with anomalies.

(d) Facilitating **"Spatial and Temporal"** activity i.e. **(Space and Time)**, to reply with accuracy of execution.

(e) **"To define skill"**, skill being a technical proficiency, is deemed as an organised co-ordinated action and function, to deal with any ongoing situations which involves the awareness of **"Spatial"** and **"Physiological"** facilitation, especially the **"Bio-Mechanics", branch of "Physics"**, the actual mechanics of movement depending on observation and adoption to external environment and **implicated** situations, specifically feedback.

(f) **"Acquired Skill Proficiencies"**, relate to the facilitation of automated reflexes in pressure situations, so that the observation and interpretation i.e. (**autominous reflex action**)is perceived by observers to be a talented response.

(g) **(Autonomy of Soccer Techniques).** This type of advance proficiencies exemplifies the players capability to produce and execute more complex sequences of controlled play and plays to his performance, e.g. (**An "Automonous Technical Proficient" player contributes significantly towards a successful conclusion to his performance and end result.**)

Facilitation of Superior Soccer Skills

Expectation levels in the pursuit of **"Peak Performances"** relate to the **"Disciplines"** in a group reaction and interaction. The following points deserve **attention for retention.**

(a) Knowledge of your team mate's **"characteristics"** and **"idiosyncrasies"**.

(b) Acquiring proficient **(skills)**.

(c) Processes involved in executing **those (skills)**.

(d) Selected feedback—**responses**.

(e) Execution, decision, processing.

(f) **Practice, correction practice** of proficiencies.

"Summary"

Open skill practice to devise and alternate activities which features all of this books exclusive **"skill proficiencies"**—INTRODUCTION OF PROFESSIONAL SOCCER SKILLS.

BALL CONTROL IN SOCCER

Trapping the ball

1.

2.

BE IN CONTROL

Trap the ball
stay focussed

Left, trapping with the
inside of the foot

TRI-VISUAL AWARENESS

3.

4

Right: trapping with the outside of the foot and moving off in the same action

Side foot pass along the ground after trapping

BE FOCUSSED—TOTAL CONCENTRATION

BALL CONTROL

DRIBBLING POINTERS:
1. Focus on your centre of gravity, i.e. balance
2. Focus on your co-ordinates, i.e. (eye) (foot) (ball).
3. Control the ball for decision making.

STAY BALANCED

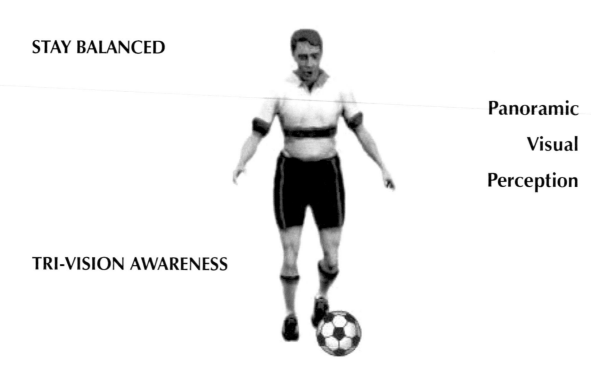

Panoramic Visual Perception

TRI-VISION AWARENESS

MONITOR OTHER PLAYERS MOVEMENTS

TECHNIQUES:
4. A skilful player controls the ball automatically.
5. A skilful player monitors other players and facets of play.
6. Facilitate "Tri-Vision" i.e. (eye) (foot) co-ordination.
7. Monitoring your team mates position, and your opponents.

STAY COOL

HEADING THE BALL

Heading is also a question of balance, in order to head properly you have to be able to jump properly and then land well balanced, ready for the next move in the game.

1. Attack the ball

2. Flick-on header

STAY BALANCED

For the most part it's the forehead you use to head the ball, no other part of the head, feel confident about it.

BE CONFIDENT

The only time you'll use the top of your head is for flick ons. This is a question of timing. It's almost like tossing your head back to clear some hair out of your eye or backward heading.

3. Downward header

4. Backward header

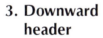

BE FOCUSSED

You have to relax when you're heading. If you are tense then the head dips and shoulders are hunched and you lose focus.

CONCENTRATE ON DIRECTION OF BALL REMEMBER: TRI VISION AWARENESS IS A PRE-REQUISITE

HEADING THE BALL

POINTERS BEFORE CONTACT:

1. Adjust your base of support for the jump
2. Ball—eye—co-ordination, keep your eyes focussed.
3. Try to always use your forehead on contact.

Be aware of Atmospheric Conditions

STAY FOCUSSED

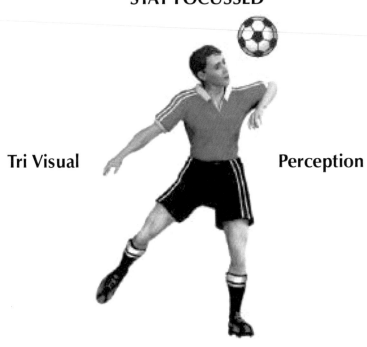

Tri Visual   Perception

STAY BALANCED

TECHNIQUES:

4. Focus on the flight of the ball, before contact
5. Assess and be aware of opponents contact
6. Control the ball and prepare for anomalies
7. Concentrate to applicate.

BE AWARE OF CONTACT IMPACT COLLISION

KICKING THE BALL

Whenever you practise your kicking use both feet. Most players favour Kicking with one foot over the other but you have to work on your weaker leg.

1. Kicking with the full instep
2. Kicking with the side of the foot
3. Knee over ball to keep shot down
4. Volley the ball – stay balanced
5. Side-foot shot – stay balanced

**CONCENTRATE
TRI-VISION AWARENESS**

TYPES OF KICKS

POINTERS—BEFORE CONTACT WITH THE BALL:
1. Address your approach positions
2. Assess the speed and movement of the ball!
3. Adjust your base of support, bio-mechanically.
4. Your success depends entirely on impact and follow-through.

STAY BALANCED

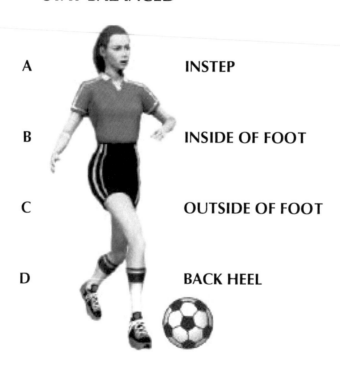

A — INSTEP
B — INSIDE OF FOOT
C — OUTSIDE OF FOOT
D — BACK HEEL

STAY IN FOCUS

TECHNIQUES:
5. Tri-Vision, i.e. (eye) (foot) co-ordination is essential.
6. Focus your intentions on impact.
7. Monitor the distance of your pass requirement.
8. Facilitate your movements autonomously.

TIMING IS A PRE-REQUISITE FOR A SUCCESSFUL CONCLUSION

CONTROLLING THE BALL WITH YOUR CHEST

TRI-VISUAL PERCEPTION

1.

Arch your back
Concave your chest

2. Forward moving chest trap

BE FOCUSSED

Monitor your team mates position as well as your opponents.

Trapping at speed, while running

Arch your back

Relay the ball

3. Receive the ball on the top of your chest

to your feet

STAY BALANCED
BALL CONTROL ESSENTIAL

THROW-INS

Correct Technique for A,B,C,D,E, Illustrations

A

Arch back, flex knees, keep both feet on the ground.

Knees must be bent, with the body forward stretching to height and distance rather than power and velocity.

B

C

When throwing, you have to remember that both feet have to be on the ground when the ball leaves both your hands, both feet have to be behind the line, and your arms have to come from behind your head and go over your head.

Short throw

D

Long throw from standing position

1. Arch your back
2. Flex your knees

E

Extra long throw fuelled by long run up and fully body action

SECTION 6

TECHNICAL PROFICIENCES FOR SOCCER

SELF-ASSESSMENT

FACILITATING A NEW MODE OF SOCCER TECHNIQUES

ELITE FITNESS FOR EXCELLENCE

EVADING A TACKLER

POINTERS: Step to one side:
1. Be aware of approach perimeters.
2. Feign to go one way and go the other way, accelerate.
3. Control the ball, use Tri-Vision Awareness.

STAY BALANCED

Panoramic Vision

Tri-Vision Perception

STAY FOCUSSED

TECHNIQUES:
4. Control the ball, (eye) (foot) co-ordination.
5. Use both outside and inside of feet for control.
6. Change your base of support for balance.
7. Accelerate away from the tackler.

CONTINUITY AFTER AVOIDING THE TACKLE

STEP AROUND A DEFENDER

POINTERS:
1. Assess your opponents position and speed of approach.
2. Control the ball firmly, using (eye) (foot) co-ordination.
3. Adjust your feet position and base of support for balance.

CHANGE DIRECTION

Panoramic Vision

Tri-Vision Awareness

Step aside

STAY FOCUSSED

TECHNIQUES
4. Step to one side of the tackle, accelerate away.
5. Change direction, look for support players.
6. Lower your centre of gravity to prepare for contact.
7. Control the ball using (eye) (foot) co-ordination.

BE SMART

AVOIDING THE TACKLER

POINTERS:
1. Assess your approach perimeters.
2. Prepare to deceive your opponent.
3. Facilitate—"Tri Vision Awarenes" (eye) (foot) and (field position)

STAY BALANCED

TRI-VISION   PANORAMIC VISION

STAY IN CONTROL

TECHNIQUES:
4. Side step away from the tackler controlling the ball
5. You step away from the defender
6. Feigning to go to his right, then changing direction to his left.
7. Accelerate away, controlling the ball.

CONTINUE AFTER EVASION

"SWERVE PAST A DEFENDER"

DRIBBLING TECHNIQUES:
1. Feign to left—swerve to right, accelerate away
2. Eye—foot—co-ordination, to control the ball
3. To swerve to the left, (alternate), swerve to right.

STAY BALANCED

Control the Ball   Tri-Vision

STAY FOCUSSED

TECHNIQUES:
4. Suddenly change direction by swerving to one side.
5. Change your base of support to remain balanced.
6. Control the ball whilst in motion.
7. Be aware of your team mates and opponents position.

TRI-VISION AND PANORAMIC VISION

TACKLING SKILLS IN SOCCER

STAY DISCIPLINED

STAY BALANCED

FRONT ON TACKLE   RIGHT SIDE TACKLE

KEEP YOUR EYES ON THE BALL

TACKLING TECHNIQUES

TIME YOUR TACKLE

LEFT SIDE ON TACKLE   SLIDING TACKLE

DEFENSIVE SKILLS

LINING UP A TACKLE

BEFORE CONTACT:
ON (LEFT OR RIGHT) SIDE OF BALL CARRIER

1. Ascertain your man's movements and approach speed
2. Adjust to your interception, focus on the ball
3. Assess the situation, go for the ball, not the man!

STAY DISCIPLINED

TIME YOUR TACKLE — **STAY BALANCED**

LEFT OR RIGHT SIDE

STAY FOCUSSED

TECHNIQUES:
4. Keep your eyes on the target, i.e. (the ball)
5. Adjust your base of support and body angles
6. Keep your faculties about you, strike with precision
7. The ball is your sole target, stay focussed.

STAY IN CONTROL

FRONT ON TACKLE

LINING UP A TACKLE:
1. Measure your distance and speed of approach
2. Measure up the ball carrier, assess his intentions
3. Keep your eyes focussed on the target, i.e. the ball

STAY BALANCED

KEEP YOUR EYES  **ON THE BALL**

ACCELERATE INTO THE TACKLE

STAY DISCIPLINED

TECHNIQUES:
4. Stay in an upright position, until you make your effort.
5. Stay on your feet if at all possible.
6. Adjust your base of support for impact collision
7. Be positive in your approach, not negative.

NEGATE ATTACKERS PROGRESS

TACKLING TECHNIQUES

POINTERS BEFORE IMPACT:
1. Line up your opponent, close down his options
2. Stay upright until you make your effort
3. Accelerate into the tackle, going for the ball.

STAY FOCUSSED

TIME YOUR TACKLE

STAY BALANCED

KEEP YOUR EYE ON THE BALL

STAY DISCIPLINED

TECHNIQUES:
4. Focus on the ball, not the player
5. Tackle from in front, or either side, not BEHIND!
6. Keep your head, be disciplined, go for the ball
7. Concentration leads to a successful conclusion.

STAY BALANCED ON CONTACT

SECTION 7

SPORTS PSYCHOLOGY
FITNESS AND TRAINING

M.I.T.   MENTAL IMAGE TRAINING

M.I.P.   MENTAL IMAGE PROGRAMMING

M.I.R.   MENTAL IMAGE REHEARSAL

VISUAL PERCEPTION – THEORY

TRI-VISION v TUNNEL VISION

EXERCISE PROGRAMME

CYBERNETICS IN SPORT

HEALTH AND FITNESS

BY BERT HOLCROFT

SOCCER: PRESSURE

STRESS & TENSION AWARENESS LEVELS

As previously mentioned the coaches and players must understand that frequently individuals react differently when placed in pressure situations, i.e. in **"Contact Impact Areas"**, at times more **Cohesively and Constructively**, at other times more **Reluctantly and Cautiously**, depending on the levels of personal proficiencies achievements. The exact reaction is not always predictable, but the coach or players must make every effort to interpret the situation, understand and then cope with these reactions. Generally it is players who are most experienced in **contact impact situations**, that display less anxiety and tension, enhancing both team and individual skills and to support each other by accepting a shared responsibility for a **successful conclusion or failure!** "Stress and Pressure situations" created in a competitive environment should be encouraged and should be the prevalent essential feature of any effective training program. **"Stress and Pressure"—(Tangibles) (i.e. known), not (Intangibles) (i.e. unknown)**, are observable in contact competitions, **technical proficient** reactions and tolerance enables the players or the coach to cope with the **"Tangibles"**, it is the **"Intangibles"!** that have to be determined and managed, so that reoccurring circumstances can be managed successfully. If these anomalies are not attended to with urgency, future actions could result in promoting **(unforced errors)! Producing** fatigue syndrome, **(the precursor to promoting—"Stress")**. It is only when this **"Stress"**, is managed that the coach or players can promote a feeling of elation and satisfaction, knowing he has achieved a successful conversion process. It is well documented that **"LOCAL STRESS"**, in any format, converts itself into **"TOTAL STRESS"**, which must be avoided, to progress to **"Elitism in Soccer"**.

INTRODUCTION OF MENTAL IMAGE PERCEPTION

Coaches and players must adapt to scientific modifications to acquaint themselves with modern formulas relating to **"MENTAL IMAGERY PERCEPTION"**. **The modern formats to (M.I.T.) i.e. (Mental Imagery Training), as well as essential physiological awareness and analysis, without these combined physiological and psychological implementation "Soccer" will stay in its dormant state.** Information systems relating to advanced **Scientific and Academical principles of modern innovations, (not only physiological practices but psychological studies)**, envelope these new projections to promote otherwise non practiced perceptions to advance soccer into **futuristic era accommodating these principles of the sciences in soccer.** With advanced thinking into these latest training theories:

    (a) M.I.T. = Mental Imaginary Training

    (b) M.I.P. = Mental Imaginary Programming

(c) M.I.R. = Mental Imaginary Rehearsal

All of these new additions to **"Soccer Training"** provide new formulas and perceptions of the modernistic approach for advancement. All these accepted formats are essential to promote new technical proficiencies, i.e. **(game plans), (tactics) and (strategies)**, to transfer your **imagery perception into a projected realism**. With constant practice these new innovations will advance your perceptions specifically in **pressure situations.** "Mental Imagery Projection" must be included in your repertoire of recognised practices. Without previous acquired skills, you could not facilitate this new **"Mental Imagery projection"**, therefore the essential pre-requisite for a successful conclusion is related to your newly acquired technical proficiencies, so that your engram systems are programmed to achieve your goal, **(repetitive practice of these newly attained skills is essential)**. To create a combination of psychological and physiological programming, the knowledge of the **"Bio-mechanical" of "Physics"** come into play, the awareness factor of **"kinesology"** playing a very important factor in your endeavour to modify your acceptance of the sciences of physiology and its integration and implementation into your drills.

TRI-VISION—APPLICATIONS

"Soccer fitness", aligns itself with positional play, as well as facilitating the skills of both attack and defence. An awareness of **"Vision"**, plays an integral part of **soccer**, most soccer players are conditioned to field awareness, in the position of their choice, it is the whole concept of **"Vision"**, which needs to be promoted, for instant, a player who is a **"moderate rated participant"** projects **"Tunnel Vision!"** one dimensional awareness, i.e. **(straight ahead and only what is in front of him)**, this player must improve his conception of **"Vision!"** and try to improve his field position and awareness by facilitating and projecting **"Panoramic Vision"**. This vision improves his awareness of the **"whole conception"**, not the previous **Tunnel Vision!"** his awareness can therefore improve his value. The ultimate awareness must be **"Tri-Visual Awareness"** this ideal concept puts you in complete control of your destiny, particularly in the facilitation of **"Smart Controlled Soccer" i.e. (dribbling), (passing), (kicking), (receiving)**, especially when the ball is in motion, **(you become a skilful soccer player from an also ran!)**, you are able to dribble the ball automatically and at the same time **monitor**the movements, not only of your own team, but most important the movements of your opposing players, **"promoting space and time"**, to process sequences to successful conclusions, this is **"Tri-Vision Awareness Being Implemented"**.

ACHIEVABLE SOCCER EXCELLENCE

To achieve excellence in your endeavour, you have to implement the previous additional requirements to **(M.I.T.), (M.I.P.), (M.I.R.)**, with the **(Visual Perception Theory)**, i.e. to facilitate **(Tri-Vision Perception)**, you must encapsulate these new concepts, to further your education and application to significantly consolidate your achievements in the futuristic realms of **Soccer. To dismiss!**these new sciences and formulations, would be a negative factor in your endeavour to advance your own and your team's pursuit of **"Excellence in the skills of Soccer"**.

PRACTICE—CORRECTION—PRACTICE

You must practice these new innovations of **(M.I.P.), (M.I.T.) & (M.I.R.)**, to equate with the mental programming and rehearsals of all your previous practices, **(skills), (game plans), (ploys), (plays), (tactics)**and **strategies**, you wish to put into practice during the ensuing game, **(specifically before the game and at half time)**—these quiet moments of mental motivation of projected application, will substantiate your implementation of increased involvement in your endeavour to produce your ultimate performance, **(M.I.R.) "Mental Imagery Rehearsal"**, should predominate your pre-game rituals. **"Summary"** and reflections of **(M.I.P), (M.I.T.) and (M.I.R.)**, combined with **"Tri-Visual Perception"**.

(M.I.P), (M.I.T.) & (M.I.R.)—PROJECTIONS

(a) What you **imagine!** should be **achievable!**

(b) Meaningful interpretation of segment imagination, should be promoted.

(c) Each personal segment of imagination and significance should be dove tailed into a team implementation.

(d) Whilst facilitating **(M.I.R.)**, you should project a performance you previously **"excelled in"**, i.e. **(a performance you were proud of)**.

(e) In your perception of an end result, be positive for the full **(90 minutes)**!

(f) Distraction and lapses of concentration could significantly disrupt your imaginery projection, creating a **negative response syndrome!**

(g) In your **"Mental Imagery Rehearsal"** you must imagine, **"you are the dominant force"**.

TRI-VISUAL PERCEPTION—PROJECTION
(i.e. Promoting your impressions and expressions on the Game)

(a) Lack of implementation of these new aids plus the **"Tri-Visual Perception" theory** gives your opponent, advantages ascendancy and superiority.

(b) (M.I.T.)—**"Mental Imagery Programming"** should be exhilarating. **"Tri-Visual Perception"** is a pre-requisite, for a successful conclusion.

ANALYSIS OF VISUAL PERCEPTION

(a) **"Tunnel Vision"** equate with **"one direct visual response"**! cutting everything and everyone out, creating **"self-implicated individualism"**.

(b) **"Panoramic Vision"**, this theory improves on **"Tunnel Vision"** it expands and promotes other objects into your vision, but deflects from the **skills** and **formations** reflections, therefore closing down your options.

(c) **"Tri-Visual Perception"**, is the ultimate pre-requisite, to formulate your optimum talents into a team co-ordinate of awareness, combining, (1) Eye, foot and your own position; (2) Your team mates position; (3) Your opponents position; (4) Perimeters—awareness; (5) Your overall perception and interpretation of all movements within the field of play, which leads into a new format, **promoting** phases of **continuity** of play called THE **"CYBERNETIC THEORY OF SKILL ACQUISITION"**.

CYBERNETICS IN SOCCER

The acquisition and retention of futuristic **"soccer skills"**, and technical proficiencies, will not prevail until the skill is engraved on to your **"Engram System"**. Unless these skills are imprinted by consecutive repetitive drills to perfection, your autonomous reflex systems will not be activated. Coaches and players must understand that automated responses determine successful transactions, be reflected under pressure and stressful situations. (**Automated reflex functions of acquired skill techniques**) are the pre-requisite for success. To advance to **autonomous reflex actions**, the previous learning of (**Cognitive Associative Autonomous**) theories are advanced by a process called the **"CYBERNETIC THEORY"**. This cybernetic theory differs from the above learning phases, it is a process involving and taking into consideration the players total behavioural aspects to his (**Disciplines**) i.e. (**skills**), capacities, as well as the players and coaches ability to observe, adapt, and react to ongoing situations, involving, expressions and interpretation of changing circumstances and stimulus. **"The Cybernetic Theory"**, places greater emphasis on the players previous experiences, interpretation and assessment of ongoing situation and changes, specifically pressure and stressful circumstances, there is a philosophy that says,

IT IS NOT PRACTICE THAT MAKES "PERFECT", IT IS "PERFECT PRACTICE", CONDUCTED UNDER "PRESSURE SITUATIONS", WITH THE "APPROPRIATE FEEDBACK" THAT MAKES FOR "PERFECT".

A word of advice. It is not possible to promote these new innovations, if your **"fitness levels"**, do not equate with the **(48 pts—SOMATOGRAPH)**. The key to facilitating these new processes rely entirely on acquisition of your **(48 pts) "FITNESS SOMATOGRAPH DIPLOMA"**.

EXCERPTS FROM SPORTING REVELATIONS BOOKS
PHILOSOPHY OF COACHING

PLAYERS WINNING WAYS & COMMITMENTS PERSONAL AWARENESS & APPLICATION

1. It is essential to concentrate throughout the match. Be ready for, or to create, a new situation, anticipate your opponents moves, rectify your own mistakes. Assess your opponent's weaknesses and exploit them. Awareness.

2. Remember your opponents can only play as well as you, and the run of the game allows them—Gain early superiority and maintain it.

3. Quick repositioning both in attack and defence is imperative, especially when yours or your opponents attack has broken down. Fill In.

4. Loose-balls)—(Turnovers) etc. Execute your tackles correctly and cleanly. Defend and cover defend, when not in possession get into position, Concentrate.

5. Learn when to let the ball do the work, when to hold it, to draw the opposition and when to pass the ball. Study economy of effort, let your positional sense conserve your energy, Attention span.

6. Team spirit is a valuable asset. Dovetail your individual efforts into team work, "United you stand, divided you fall". Be Brave.

7. Make a point of understanding your team mates, both in temperament and style of play. If your colleague makes a mistake, try to cover it up, do not complain, it may be you next time. Communicate—Interchange.

8. Regard the game as a challenge to your maximum ability. And always play your hardest and best. If you're superior, don't ease off. Never give up, even when the odds are against you. Be Courageous.

9. Don't be a slave to the orthodox. Risks have to be taken but sound judgement and common sense will help you to decide when they shall be taken. Know when to hold and when to pass. Integrate.

10. Try to get a grip of the game from the kick off. Always strive for the initiative, never under estimate, or over estimate, your opponents. Be Positive.

11. Rugby is a man's game and you must be prepared to give and take hard knocks both physically and mentally. Acknowledge your own mistakes, avoid blaming the other fellow, and above all don't feel sorry for yourself. Good Attitude.

12. Respect and support officials and your captain, especially the Referee—he wants the game to be a success. Discipline.

13. Remember, never over-estimate the victory, or your own personal achievements. It takes a long time to build the reputation of a good sportsman, but you can—lose it in one game. Commitment and tolerance.

H Holcroft.

(GRADE III)
COACHING KNOWLEDGE PRINCIPLES AND APPLICATIONS

LUCK DEFINED

(A) You could interpret luck in sport as an advantage where:-

OPPORTUNITY & PREPARATION MEET

(B) Luck is always present if you have the fortitude to recognise and accept it.

(C) Luck is manufactured by your volition, i.e. attitude, presentation, dedication, application, commitment and awareness.

(D) The level of **luck** could relate to levels of tolerance.

STAY COOL

SECTION 8

SPORTS NUTRITIONAL ANALYSIS

DETERMINING THE AEROBIC AND ANAEROBIC THRESHOLD.

(A) ENERGY TO BURN
(B) CHEMICAL ENERGY
(C) PRE-GAME NUTRITIONAL ENERGY

SIMPLIFIED AND DEFINED

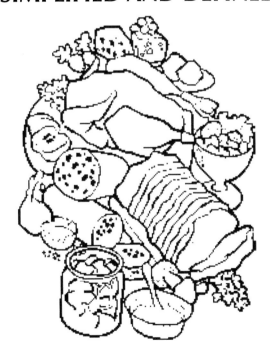

BY BERT HOLCROFT

GRADE III ACCREDITED COACH.

NUTRITIONAL GUIDELINES FOR HEALTH

The current literature on nutrition is vast and often complex. From the participant's point of view, providing no specific nutrition-related problems exist, it is more practical to follow sound eating patterns and major guidelines rather than be concerned with highly specific information.

Foods comprise three major groups—fats, proteins and carbohydrates. These three components provide all energy for the body in various combinations depending on the foods eaten. Alcohol also provides energy! **but has several side effects such as dehydration, loss of motor skill and co-ordination.**

The participant needs to place far more emphasis on carbohydrate in the diet. Generally speaking, carbohydrate should make up between 60-70% of total calorie intake for active sports people. "Carbohydrate loading" is a practice that has been advocated in some studies but it generally is most successful for activities of a continuous nature, lasting in excess of 60 minutes. For the participant, it is more prudent to simply increase overall carbohydrate intake.

NUTRITIONAL GUIDANCE FOR THE ELITE ATHLETES

The process of food assimilation biologically relates to metabolism converting the different food intake to energy and other bio-chemical forms. The three bio-chemical reactions are:

(A) **Anabolism:** The process in which food is built up into protoplasm and cell construction from carbohydrates and fat.

(B) **Catabolism:** The process in which living tissue is broken down into substrates plus A.T.P, i.e. the body's currency unit of energy.

(C) **Metabolism:** The process of A and B to produce energy.

NUTRITION SIMPLIFIED

Just simply, if your food intake produces more calories than your metabolic rate uses, the extra calories are chemically converted to other forms of energy, i.e. fat and stored as excess energy in the fat cells. This is termed Anabolism, i.e. you gain weight.

If your food intake produces less calories than your metabolic rate, stored energy, i.e. fat is converted back to calories to make up the short-fall of your metabolic rate, i.e. exercise intensity—Catabolism, you lose weight.

TO GAIN STRENGTH AND MUSCLE BULK

Food assimilation is concentrated on the protein (pre-game foods) see page 73, combined with an exercise résumé of progressive resistance, specifically weight-training forms of muscle development.

Alcohol doesn't help the participant recover from exercise, as it prolongs and exacerbates dehydration. The participant who trains on Sunday (or is involved in some other sport) has to be clever if he drinks on a Saturday night. Non-alcoholic fluid (2-3 litres) should be consumed prior to sleep and the use of low or non-alcoholic beer should be encouraged. **Attempting to play a sport in a dehydrated and sub-optimal condition is both unrewarding and dangerous and should be discouraged.**

FOOD AND FUEL FOR FITNESS

PERFORMANCE.

To perform at your optimal level, your dietary intake must be examined carefully. Why train hard if you are going to ignore what you eat? How true is the saying "You are what you eat"? If nutrition is not included as an integral part of training and sport preparation, then even the most talented participant will never reach his full potential.

Participants need to be aware of the food they eat as it gives them energy to train and play. Food is mainly made up of the following nutrition, each with a specific job.

Food Categories:
- Carbohydrates
- Food Groups.

(A) Carbohydrates.

Carbohydrates act as a form of energy source in the muscles for training and matches. Lack of carbohydrates in the diet leads to inadequate energy stores to train and play. Carbohydrates must the basis of every meal.

Source of Carbohydrates.

Wholemeal breakfast cereals, rolls, muffins, pancakes, crackers, rice, pasta, noodles, wholemeal biscuits, scones, plain popcorn, fruit—fresh or tinned, stewed or dried, juice, muesli bars, sweet spreads, vegetables, potatoes, corn, peas, low fat yogurts and milk drinks, carbohydrate drinks.

(B) Fats.

Fats act as a form of energy in long periods of activity. They supply twice as much energy as carbohydrates but are not as efficient. **Excess fat in the diet will lead to large fat stores that inhibit performance.**

Sources of fats to avoid.

Butter, margarine, oil, fatty meat, chips, savoury snacks, roasted nuts, chocolate before performance, i.e. match or training.

(C) Proteins.

Proteins act to build and repair the body. If the protein intake is too high, it will be **stored as fat.** If insufficient protein is taken then a player will fatigue, have an inability to recovery from injury and lose muscle bulk.

Sources of Protein.

Lean beef, veal, pork, lamb, skinless poultry, fish and seafood—fresh or tinned in water, eggs, soybeans, baked beans, nuts.

Common dietary concerns.

- Insufficient energy intake leading to fatigue.
- Incorrect balance of energy sources—usually too low in carbohydrates and too high in fats.
- Vitamins and mineral deficiencies—leading to poor health.
- Insufficient fluid intake—causing dehydration.

recommendations for fluid balance.

(1) Condition your body to get used to taking fluids, by using fluids during training sessions. Water or a correctly-mixed carbohydrate drink is ideal. Too often, carbohydrate drinks are mixed incorrectly and result in dehydration rather than hydration. Carbohydrate drinks can replenish loss of fluid while also providing additional carbohydrates to supplement the body's energy reserves. Small amounts and often is the rule.

(2) Make sure that you are fully hydrated before participating in training or a match.

(3) Take 250-500mls of water 20 to 40 minutes before any training or match.

(4) Following exercise, **start rehydration immediately.**

(5) At half time, drink glucose and water, not **acidic or fizzy drinks.**

Supplements.

The body also needs certain vitamins and minerals (A, C, E), are the main anti-oxidants.

Vitamin C—Citrus and tropical fruit, vegetables.

B Vitamins—Wholegrain bread and cereals, brown rice and pastas, dairy products, lean meat.

Vitamin A—Fruit and vegetables, eggs, dairy products and margarine.

Iron—Organ meats, e.g. liver, beef and other meats, turkey, chicken and fish.

Calcium—dairy products.

On the training days, there are two main nutritional requirements.

energy

hydration

Energy should come from complex carbohydrate such as found in pasta, rice, potatoes etc. Protein and fats take a considerable period of time to become available (the normal varied diet contains two to three times the daily requirement of protein, negating any need for protein supplements). This meal should occur between 2-4 hours before training. However, this is variable depending on individual tolerance to food.

Hydration is a vital factor. Thirst is a very poor indicator of water need. You should drink well before feeling thirsty. **Dehydration will markedly affect performance.** Plain water or diluted glucose drink is best before and during training, especially so if it can be taken cold as this accelerates the rate of absorption.

After training, it is **vital to rehydrate** by drinking either plain water or replacements in the form of liquid carbohydrate for the first hour post-training. Additionally, a small quantity of carbohydrate in the first 30 minutes after exercise has been shown to markedly decrease recovery time and help re-synthesis of damaged tissue.

THE DEMON DRINK

SPORTS PARTICIPATION & THE EFFECTS OF ALCOHOL

Alcohol consumption is part of the post-match social aspects of many sporting events. Alcohol, however, is a drug and excessive or inappropriate use of this drug can be a cause of both short-term and long-term morbidity.

The Effects of Alcohol on Athletic Performance.

Rugby football, like all other athletic pursuits, requires the expenditure of energy. The energy to contract muscles and thus move the body can be produced in two ways, either aerobically or anaerobically.

1. Aerobic Energy Production

Aerobic energy is the energy used for stamina exercise. Aerobic energy is produced with the use of oxygen. This type of energy is utilised in activities, which take place over a period of minutes. A rugby example of aerobic exercise would be the constant motion of the scrum half and back row forwards throughout the 80 minutes of a match. Similarly, the referee will be involved in aerobic exercise throughout the rugby match.

2. Anaerobic Exercise.

Anaerobic exercise does not utilise oxygen and takes place over a much shorter time period (seconds). It is the short, sharp energy which rugby players use when hitting a ruck, pushing in a scrum or jumping in the line out. Tackling an opponent or sprinting with the ball are also examples of anaerobic exercise.

It is always difficult to accurately determine the energy source requirements (aerobic or anaerobic) in a team game, especially a collision game like rugby football. However, it is concluded that the forwards need a high stamina capacity as the majority of their work is aerobic—a rugby forward will on average cover three miles in a game. The ability to cover this ground quickly will often determine how he plays. Forwards also need to develop their anaerobic energy source particularly for scrummaging, rucking and line-out jumping.

Alcohol has a high calorific content as a 12oz can of beer contains 150 calories but only 50 are in the form of carbohydrate. The majority of the remaining calories in a 12oz can of beer are from the alcohol content. These are not converted into glycogen and therefore do not replace depleted glycogen stores. **Alcohol is not the most appropriate way of replacing depleted carbohydrate stores.**

Sensible Drinking.

If the rugby player wishes to drink alcohol after his game, he should first ensure that he rehydrates with glucose and electrolyte-containing drinks. Water is also adequate for rehydration but does not contain sufficient electrolyte or carbohydrate. Two or three litres of fluid after a game will replace sweat losses and will also help to **stave off the dehydration which alcohol may produce.**

Thirsty rugby players should not use alcohol as their first drink post exercise. Drinking beer in the dressing room is definitely out as this is when players are at their most dehydrated. Ideally the players should drink carbohydrates and electrolyte-rich drinks as soon as they come off the pitch and prior to showering. This is the time when the carbohydrate stores are at their most depleted and are easily replenished.

Alcohol does not help the player recover from exercise, as it prolongs and exacerbates dehydration. The player who trains on Sunday (or is involved in some other sport) has to be clever if he drinks on a Saturday night. Non-alcoholic fluid (2-3 litres) should be consumed prior to sleep and the use of low or non-alcoholic beer should be encouraged. **Attempting to play a sport in a dehydrated and sub—optimal condition is both unrewarding and dangerous and should be discouraged.**

Conclusion.

Alcohol can be a pleasant form of relaxation after a rugby match. It should, however, be treated with respect. Alcohol can be a cause of both short-term and long-term morbidity and in a few sad cases can be associated with dependence.

Alcohol is not the athlete's best friend. It does not enhance performance and its hangover effects diminish aerobic performance. It is not physiologically suitable as a rehydrating or fuel agent.

It is therefore incumbent on those associated with sport to educate players regarding the effects of alcohol upon health and physical performance.

Food Percentages: Pre-training & Pre-match.

The recommended energy distribution for a rugby player is:

1. At least **55-60% Carbohydrate.**
2. Less than **30% from fat.**
3. **12-15% Protein.**

Food intake before training and matches.

1. Eat at least **2 to 3 hours** before training or a game.
2. **Cut fat, protein and high fibre foods intake** to a minimum.
3. Boiled or stewed foods assist in the digestive process, rather than fried or roasted. **A big fry-up** is not recommended **on the morning of a match.**

Food intake after training and matches.

1. Eat **high carbohydrate** food immediately after training or a game. It can be the least favourable time for some players but it is the most beneficial. Always keep a supply of **carbohydrate foods in your kit bag,** i.e. fruit, carbohydrate drink for after the session.
2. Drink **carbohydrate drinks or water** to balance fluids lost.
3. **Fluid must be replaced after training or matches.** Alcohol is not a fluid supplement. It affects the body **72 hours** after intake. **Alcohol also disrupts your co-ordination, making it dangerous to train.**

Pre-Training and Pre-Competition Needs.

Drink water before, during and after workouts.

✎ A word about food prior to **competition** and hard **workouts.**

1. **No fats or "thick meats"** for at least **4 hours prior to events.**
2. **Heavy amounts of liquids** only up to ½-¾ hour before.
3. **"Light snacks",** e.g. salad, up to 1-1 1¼ hours before.
4. **Use of pre-digested, replacement foods** up to ¾-1 hour before.

Sensible nutritional habits before training or competition will avoid unnecessary discomfort and improve performance. **Too much food in the stomach** at the start of a game may produce a bloated, uncomfortable sensation and may lead to cramps or diarrhoea.

The old **"steak and eggs"** pre-match meal may take up to **6 hours to digest** and yet some still continue with this practice before the afternoon's competition!

MATCH-DAY NUTRITION

1. **Do not** eat a fried breakfast.
2. **Do not** overload your digestive tract.
3. **Do not** eat fatty foods.
4. **Do not** eat protein foods.
5. **Do not** drink fluid and eat food at the same time.
6. **Do** eat carbohydrate food.
7. **Do** eat fruit combinations.
8. **Do** drink water or glucose.
9. **Do not** drink milk.
10. **Do not** become dehydrated.
11. You must **not feel hungry!**
12. You must **feel strong** nutritionally.
13. Resist from **food** intake for at least **2½ hours** before competing.
14. **To simplify, correct combinations of nutritious food are recommended.**

CARE OF COMMON SPORT INJURIES

Ankle Sprains.
- Apply ice immediately.
- Keep off the affected limb.
- If unable to take weight on it next day, seek medical advice.

Cauliflower Ear.
- Apply ice immediately.
- Apply compression bandage.
- If you don't get it drained in the first 24 hours, future treatment is less than successful.

Torn Hamstring.
- Do not play on with a hamstring injury.
- Apply ice immediately to the tender area of the hamstring.
- After 2 days, physiotherapy and gentle stretching exercises will speed up recovery.
- Proper warm-up to prevent hamstring tears is far better than trying to treat

them when they have torn.

Cuts and Scrapes.
- After showering, apply some antiseptic and cover wound with a dressing.
- Cover shin wounds before playing or training again.
- If wound is deep or bleeding profusely, then seek medical advice.

Bangs to the Head and Concussion.
- Any player who has been knocked out, even for a moment, should not continue playing and should be accompanied to hospital by a responsible adult.
- If a player who has had a bang to the head during a match and is not knocked out but gets groggy or disorientated afterwards should also attend the nearest casualty department.
- Safety regulations dictate that any player suffering from concussion should not participate in any match or training session for at least 3 weeks from the time of injury.

Remember Prevention.
- Gumshields, shinguards, warm-up and proper fitness.
- Tetanus injections should be kept up-to-date.

ESSENTIAL NUTRITIONAL GUIDELINES FOR FAT LOSS—SOMATOTYPE

Weight loss should come from the fat stores in the body.
Losing only fat weight will help to ensure physical efficiency. The amount of fat weight that needs to be lost must be determined by evaluating the body's fat content.

Fat percentages for Backs = 10%-12%. For Forwards -13%-18%.

WARNING

SMOKING IS A HEALTH HAZARD

This advice is well documented by Government Health Authorities.

SMOKING CAUSES LUNG CANCER

Smoking is also a DETRIMENT TO ALL TYPES OF PHYSICAL PERFORMANCE

Every coach and participant in sport should take heed of this information

SMOKING AFFECTS YOUR FUTURE

As a COACH or MENTOR, you SHOULD INSIST that all of your charges

ABSTAIN from SMOKING.

SMOKING IS DETRIMENTAL TO YOUR SUCCESS

SECTION 9

SELF ASSESSMENT

A. SCIENTIFIC TESTING
B. FITNESS ANALYSIS FOR SPORT

A. NINE COMPONENTS

B. FIVE INTENSITY LEVELS

C. FOUR FITNESS GRADES

APPLIED KINESIOLOGY

BY BERT HOLCROFT

SCIENTIFIC & FITNESS REVELATIONS.

A. FITNESS ANALYSIS FOR SPORT

OPTIMUM (48 TEST) FITNESS ANALYSIS.

Mod optimum (Test 48) Personal Fitness Somatograph. If 100% is achieved by any first-grade squad, it would give that team the edge over the opposition. Personal Specific Progress Resistance Chart.

INTRODUCTION.

SCIENTIFIC TESTING.

An individual training programme should be issued to each player. The player should be given a training card on which he details his participation in a particular discipline, i.e. weights, endurance, plyo-dynamics, etc. Groups of players should be allocated a "Fitness Monitor", who periodically checks to ensure that his players are adhering to their training schedule.

A plyo-dynamic session could be conducted on a separate night under the supervision of your Coach, consisting of various bounding, leaping and jumping exercises.

A fitness-assessment week should be conducted under the guidance of your coaching co-ordinator, culminating in a full day's tests. Each player should be then given his personal fitness chart showing his strengths, weaknesses and a programme to correct the weaknesses.

As the season progresses, training should be stepped up, with more emphasis being place on ball work, but each player should still also maintain his personal fitness level. Intermittent tests should be conducted *every month* for the first *3 months*, thereafter every *two months* to the end of the season, until the optimum (48pts) has been attained by *every player* in your squad.

(Fitness Assessor)
Coaching Co-ordinator
Course Co-ordinator
Bert Holcroft

INTRODUCTION

OPTIMUM (48 TEST) FITNESS ANALYSIS

This fitness-conditioning regime has been proven clinically and approved by **exercise physiologists** as an optimum program to attain peak fitness and condition to play **all relevant sports**. In regards to **upper and lower body strengths**, you would have get an exercise physiologist to program a **Personal Specific Progressive Resistance Chart,** i.e. **(individual weight training)** and combine these two fitness and conditioning programs with a **Plyo-dynamic Résumé Program.**

POWER AEROBIC. EXERCISE TARGET HEART PULSE RATE EASY-TO-READ INTENSITY GRAPH.

Base Heart rate = 60 beats per minute.

Pulse 220 minus age	% Max.	Heart beats	Maximum	Exercise Intensive
Sample 220-20= 200 b.p.m.	Heart rate	Target zone per minute	Heart rate	Zone
20 years	60%	Sustain 120 b.p.m.	200 b.p.m.	Min. 30 minutes
20 years	85%	Sustain 170 b.p.m.	200 b.p.m.	30 minutes
25 years	60%	Sustain 117 b.p.m.	195 b.p.m.	Min. 30 minutes
25 years	85%	Sustain 166 b.p.m.	195 b.p.m.	30 minutes.

Graph-Age related % zones. Percentage of maximum heart rates.

Intensity percentage—60% to 80% of your age-related target heart pulse-rate. Warm-up, warm-down.

To check the pulse rate count, place the first finger on the wrist radial artery. Count pulse-rate at rest (Base pulse-rate = 60 beats per minute).

Example: Beats 10 in 6 seconds = 6 x 10 = 60 beats per minute.

CHART SPEED TESTS (Bert Holcroft)

Timed.

(A) Timed over selected distance.

Start Positions.

(B) Standing or Crouch start.

Wearing Apparel (Footwear).

(C) Shoes, boots or spikes.

Adjudicators.

(D) Two officials start and finish.

Chart Reference for Tests 1-5.

1. Mile distance—time 6 minutes.
2. Fifty yards (T=Track) (F=Field),   50 yards, T or F.
3. One Hundred yards   100 yards, T or F.
4. Two Hundred yards   200 yards, T or F.
5. Six Hundred yards   600 yards, T or F.

Variations of Speed Tests.

(1). Time each (10 yards) of (50 yards)=(2) Time last (30 yards) of (100 yards).

1. Anaerobic Tests.
2. Aerobic Test to be run in one separate session.

AFTER WARM-UP AND STRETCHING.
FIELD TEST FOR AEROBIC CAPACITY SIMPLIFIED.
OXYGEN UPTAKE CAPACITY TESTS.
CHART OF AEROBIC FITNESS (5-MILE TEST) (TARGET 30 MINS.)
F=FAIL, G=GOOD, VG=VERY GOOD, P= PASS.

This test is similar to the **5-mile aerobic fitness run,** except that here you can fairly accurately predict your maximum oxygen uptake capacity. Take the test on a **440—yard running track** or on a level course of known length (must be grass).

To pass the test, you need to score a 7, 8, 9, 10, 11 or 12.

		AEROBIC FITNESS CHART			
		OXYGEN COST PROFILES			
		RUNNING SPEED (M.P.H.)	MILE-PACE MINS. – SECS.	OXYGEN COST Ml / Kg / Mins.	POINTS
F	1	6:00	10:00	33:30	0
F	2	6:50	9:14	36:30	0
F	3	7:00	8:34	39:40	0
F	4	7:50	8:00	42:40	1
G	5	8:00	7:30	45:60	2
G	6	8:50	7:04	48:60	2½
VG	7	9:00	6:40	51:80	3
VG	8	9:50	6:19	55:10	3½
P	9	10:00	6:00	58:20	4
P	10	10:50	5:43	61:50	5
P	11	11:00	5:27	64:80	6
P	12	11:50	5:10	68:10	7
A 6-minute mile (Section 9) is acceptable.					
Level of Fitness of Aerobic Capacity.					
SUITABLE FIELD TESTS FOR ACCURACY.					

FITNESS TEST GRIDS: CONT (6-12)

HOPS — 6, 7

SIT-UPS BENT KNEE — 8

FULL PRESS-UPS — 9

BOUNDING — 10

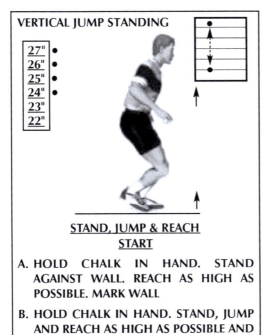

VERTICAL JUMP STANDING

27"
26"
25"
24"
23"
22"

STAND, JUMP & REACH START

A. HOLD CHALK IN HAND. STAND AGAINST WALL. REACH AS HIGH AS POSSIBLE. MARK WALL

B. HOLD CHALK IN HAND. STAND, JUMP AND REACH AS HIGH AS POSSIBLE AND MARK WALL ABOVE ORIGINAL MARK.

C. MEASURE DISTANCE BETWEEN 1ST MARK AND 2ND MARK

VERTICAL JUMP – THREE STEP

27"
26"
25"
24"
23"
22"

TAKE THREE STEPS, JUMP AND REACH

TO CONVERT:

1. Inches to cm x by (2.54)
2. Yards to metres x by (0.9144)
3. One mile = (1.609 kilometres)

SOMATOGRAPH ASSESSMENT TESTS

OPTIMUM (48 TEST) FITNESS ANALYSIS – *Accreditation* – PERSONAL FITNESS SOMATOGRAPH

NAME				AGE		% BODY FAT				DATE(S) TESTED			
3 MILES	600 YDS	200 YDS	100 YDS	50 YDS	BOUND 50 YDS	5 LEFT-FOOT HOPS	5 RIGHT-FOOT HOPS	60 SEC SIT-UPS	60 SEC PRESS-UPS	VERTICAL JUMP			
										STANDING	3 STEP		
1	2	3	4	5	6	7	8	9	10	11	12		
MINUTES	MIN / SEC	SECONDS	SECONDS	SECONDS	NUMBER	LENGTH	LENGTH	NUMBER	NUMBER	HEIGHT			
18 – **P**↑	1 - 35	25.50	11.30	5.50	18	45'	45'	60	65	24"	26"		
19 – **P**↑	1 - 40	26.00	11.80	6.10	19	43'	43'	55	60	23"	24"		
20 – **A**→	1 - 45	26.50	12.50	6.50	20	40'	40'	50	50	22"	23"		
21 – **F**↓	1 - 50	27.00	12.80	6.80	21	36'	36'	45	48	21"	22"		
22 – **F**↓	1 - 55	27.50	13.10	7.10	22	33'	33'	39	46	20"	21"		
23 – **F**↓	2 - 00	28.00	13.40	7.40	23	30'	30'	37	44	19"	20"		
24 – **F**↓	2 - 05	28.50	13.70	7.70	24	29'	29'	35	43	18"	19"		
3 MILES	600 YDS	200 YDS	100 YDS	50 YDS	BOUND 50 YDS	5 LEFT-FOOT HOPS	5 RIGHT-FOOT HOPS	60 SEC SIT-UPS	60 SEC PRESS-UPS	VERTICAL JUMP			

P = Pass
A = Average
F = Fail

TO CONVERT: 1. Inches to cm x by (2.54)   2. Yards to metres x by (0.9144)   3. One mile = (1.609 kilometres)

SOMATOGRAPH ASSESSMENT TESTS

PERSONAL FITNESS ASSESSMENT CHART (48 PTS) SOMATOGRAPH TEST.

	NAME	POSITION	AGE	DATE OF TEST	
	TWELVE DISCIPLINES	PERSONAL GRID TIME	PASS – EX GRID TIME	P = PASS F = FAIL	
1	3 miles – Aerobic	< 20 mins	> 18 mins	3 4	**4**
2	600 yds – anaerobic	1 mins 40 secs	1 min 35 secs	3 4	**4**
3	200 yds – anaerobic	26.5 secs	25.5 secs	3 4	**4**
4	100 yds – anaerobic	12.3 secs	11.3 secs	3 4	**4**
5	50 yds – anaerobic	6.00 secs	5.5 secs	3 4	**4**
6	5 right-foot hops Power & Agility	43 ft	45 ft	3 4	**4**
7	5 left-foot hops Power & Agility	43 ft	45 ft	3 4	**4**
8	60 seconds Full sit-ups	No. 55	No. 60	3 4	**4**
9	60 seconds Full press-ups	No. 60	No. 65	3 4	**4**
10	50 yds – bounding	No. 19	No. 18	3 4	**4**
11	Stand vertical jump Power & Leg strength	23 inches	24 inches	3 4	**4**
12	3-step vertical jump. Power and leg strength	25 inches	26 inches	3 4	**4**
					48.P

The above chart as been formulated for 18 to 36 age group.

ELITE ATHLETES: CONDITIONING PROGRAMME.

Aerobic and anaerobic age-related heart predictions (**R.H.R**) to (**M.H.R**), i.e. (**T.H.R**). Your work-rate input is determined by your age relating to **maximum heart-rate predictions** and training résumé. (**Refer to your R.H.R 65 b.p.m.**) (T.H.R. = Target Heart Rate).

Example: A 27-year-old athlete's work rate would be a maximum of **220 b.p.m.—27 years** equated with a pulse rate of **193 b.p.m. Hypothetical Resting Heart Rate (R.H.R) 65 b.p.m.**

Heart-Rate Reserve (H.R.R.)

To exercise above this pulse rate, i.e. **193 b.p.m to 220 b.p.m.** could be dangerous! To determine your own age-related target heart-pulse rate, take your age (**in this example 27**) from **220 b.p.m. (193 b.p.m.)** to determine your **Target Heart Rate of 75-85%** of your **T.H.R.**

Your hypothetical pulse rate at rest (**R.H.R.**) = 65 b.p.m. To determine your intensity of training:

(193−65=128 b.p.m)=(75%!128)+(65 b.p.m.)=161 b.p.m.=lower rate of intensity exercise. To improve **your aerobic capacity** and increase your anaerobic threshold, increase your exercise
intensity to (85% x 128 b.p.m.)+ 65 b.p.m (173-80) b.p.m. Your target heart-rate
   108.80 b.p.m
zone, **for at least 30 minutes of activity without rest.**

Repeated exercise résumé using your target heart-rate zone exercise intensity will produce a far greater and more efficient cardiovascular-respiratory functional capacity than any other activity.

Example:—27 year old = Lowest intensity—(161 b.p.m !173.80 b.p.m).

Highest M.H.R. predictions for 30 minutes' aerobic intensity exercises.

CARDIOVASCULAR ENDURANCE CAPACITY.

To improve your endurance levels, you must cultivate your cardiovascular-respiratory functional capacity—that is to create a greater ($\cdot VO_2max$) equates with (**The volume of oxygen uptake**)=(**per ml / kg / min) of exercise**—to increase the levels of your aerobic and anaerobic threshold levels. Other ways to increase your endurance is to run a measured distance i.e. **1 mile** inside a stipulated time of **6 minutes** or **2 miles x 12 minutes** or **3 miles x 18 minutes**. Please convert to kilometres, do not run on hard surfaces.

THIS EXERCISE-INTENSITY PREDICTION OF (58.20 $\cdot VO_2$—MAX), AN ACCEPTED LEVEL OF "CARDIOVASCULAR RESPIRATORY FUNCTIONAL CAPACITY".

Sports Coaching

Olympic Aerobic Circuit Eight Station Excercises

Olympic Aerobic Fitness Circuit Programme for the Masses

Course Director
Margo Holcroft

Course Director
Bert Holcroft

Working in partnership with Sports Revelation Enterprises   Donald A. Chu, Ph.D.   Copyright © 2008 Sports Revelation Enterprises, all rights reserved.
Email: bert@sportsrevent.com

Sports Coaching

Olympic Aerobic Circuit Eight Station Excercises

Help each other achieve the 8 exercises in family groups, pairs or singular. DO NOT RACE

1. Walk and Jog this circuit for WARM UP
2. After deep breathing exercises go to S8
3. Start stretching exercises
   - Gentle stretches
   - Do not bounce up and down
   - When at FULL stretch hold for 5-10 seconds
   - Upper and Lower body stretches
4. Go through stations S1 to S8
   - Breathe in and out normally during exercise
   - NEVER hold your breathe
5. WARM DOWN
   - by walking and jogging the circuit again
6. S8 - Finish with stretching exercises

NOTE;
We suggest when starting exercises you do 5 of each, increase the number each time you exercise. By increasing your drills you effect a "Progressive Resistance Exercise Regime"

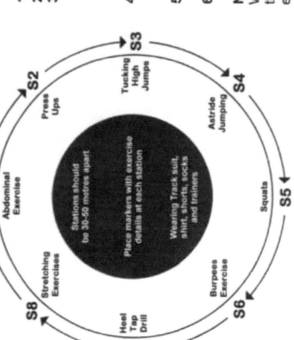

Donald A. Chu, Ph.D.   Copyright © 2008 Sports Revelation Enterprises, all rights reserved.

Working in partnership with Sports Revelation Enterprises
Email: bert@sportsrevent.com

Sports Coaching

Olympic Aerobic Circuit
Station 1 - Abdominal Exercises

CALISTHENICS FOR WARM-UP ABDOMINALS

SIT-UPS WITH BENT KNEES

LOWER BODY

Side Stomach (external obliques) These protect against internal injuries

TWIST TO LEFT & RIGHT TOUCH KNEE WITH OPPOSITE ELBOW

UPPER BODY

Working in partnership with Sports Revelation Enterprises   Donald A. Chu, Ph.D.   Copyright © 2008 Sports Revelation Enterprises, all rights reserved.
Email: bert@sportsrevent.com

Sports Coaching

Olympic Aerobic Circuit
Station 2 - Press Up Exercise

MOBILITY AND STRENGTH

DO NOT HOLD YOUR BREATH DURING EXERCISE

UPPER BODY

PUSH - UPS

Breathe steadily
Complete a regular number (start with 5)

This will increase the strength and endurance in shoulder and chest muscles.

Working in partnership with Sports Revelation Enterprises   Donald A. Chu, Ph.D.   Copyright © 2008 Sports Revelation Enterprises, all rights reserved.
Email: bert@sportsrevent.com

Sports Coaching

Olympic Aerobic Circuit
Station 3 - Tucking High Jump

LOWER BODY

Tucking High Jump

Provides exercise for heart and lungs, development of power in the legs and a mobility exercise for the spine and hips. Agility and mobility.

**TUCKING HIGH JUMP
AGILITY AND MOBILITY
FOR THIGHS AND LOWER BACK**

Working in partnership with Sports Revelation Enterprises   Donald A. Chu, Ph.D.   Copyright © 2008 Sports Revelation Enterprises, all rights reserved.
Email: bert@sportsrevent.com

Sports Coaching

Olympic Aerobic Circuit
Station 4 - Astride Jump

CALISTHENICS FOR WARM UP CIRCUIT

LOWER BODY

Astride Jumping - Agility & Mobility (minimum 20 repetitions)

This develops power in the legs and is a mobility exercise for the hips.

ASTRIDE JUMPING

Sports Coaching

Olympic Aerobic Circuit
Station 5 - Squats (bent knees)

LOWER BODY

Squats (lower body)

Strengthens the thigh muscles. Muscular strength.

**SQUATS
MUSCULAR
STRENGTH FOR
HIPS AND THIGHS.**

Working in partnership with Sports Revelation Enterprises   Donald A. Chu, Ph.D.   Copyright © 2008 Sports Revelation Enterprises, all rights reserved.
Email: bert@sportsrevent.com

Sports Coaching

Olympic Aerobic Circuit
Station 6 - Burpees Exercise

UPPER AND LOWER BODY

Burpees (upper & lower body)
For stamina and suppleness, endurance and agility.

BURPEES - 4 COUNT

Working in partnership with Sports Revelation Enterprises   Donald A. Chu, Ph.D.   Copyright © 2008 Sports Revelation Enterprises, all rights reserved.
Email: bert@sportsrevent.com

Sports Coaching

Olympic Aerobic Circuit
Station 7 - Heels Up & Speed Drills

LOWER BODY

Drill 1: High Knees - Speed Drill

Develops the muscles for a fast, long stride and adds flexibility in the hamstrings.

Pump arms vigorously.
Do not pump hands
Above shoulder level.

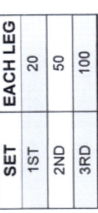

SET	EACH LEG
1ST	20
2ND	50
3RD	100

Drill 2: Heel Ups

Develops strength in the hamstring and active flexibility in quadriceps.

TAP HEELS WITH HANDS

SET	EACH LEG
1ST	20
2ND	50
3RD	100

BREATHE NORMALLY DURING EXERCISE

Donald A. Chu, Ph.D.

Copyright © 2008 Sports Revelation Enterprises, all rights reserved.

Working in partnership with Sports Revelation Enterprises
Email: bert@sportsrevent.com

Sports Coaching

Olympic Aerobic Circuit
Station 8 - All Sports Stretching

HEALTH & FITNESS CIRCUIT

UPPER BODY

1) Oblique - Upper Lat Stretch

2) Quadricep Stretch

3) Hip Flexor Stretch

5) Basic Lower Back & Groin Area

LOWER BODY

4) Hamstring Stretch

6) Hip Flexor & Groin Area

MUSCLE STRETCHES LEFT & RIGHT SIDE

7) Left Side — Abductor Stretch

Working in partnership with Sports Revelation Enterprises   Donald A. Chu, Ph.D.   Copyright © 2008 Sports Revelation Enterprises, all rights reserved.
Email: bert@sportsrevent.com

THE SCIENTIFIC TRAINING PROGRAMME
"PRE GAME FITNESS SOMATOGRAPH"

We consider that the present **'Pre Game warm up Format'** as in adequate to bring an **'Aerobic fitness Conditioning Programme'** to a successful conclusion.

We have designed an **'Aerobic Fitness Conditioning Formula'** that would facilitate an **'Adequate Aerobic Pre Game Fitness Conditioning Warm Up For All Sports'**.

We termed it **A.R.T.H.E.R.s** quest **ie; (Age Related Target Heart Exercise Rate)**. By using specific Drills leading up to **(60%) of A.R.T.H.E.R s quest**, each player test their own **'Pulse Rate'** at intervals via their **'Wrist Radial Artery'**, counting to **(6 and multiplied by 10) to equate with (60 beats per minute) maintain for 20 to 30 min's.**

Check Result of Count against your **"Age Related Target Heart Pulse Rate Chart"**, and **Increase your Intensity** until each individual player reaches the required **(60%)**, of their **'Age Related Target Heart Exercise Rate'** the main target is eventually **(80%) of A.R.T.H.E.R. s 'Fitness Plateau'**.

This Plateau must be attained to promote an elite Performance Activating their **'Attention Span + Retention Span + Awareness Span'** throughout the **80 min's** of an **'Intensive, Expressive game of Continuity Rugby'** from the start + during the latter stages of a game to the Finish.

Only then can Teams put in to practice **ploy's + play's** Formulating and implementing their Coaches **'Strategies, Tactics and Game plans'** they have spent week's of practicing to achieve **'Winning ways'** implementing a **"Successful Conclusion"**.

ELITE ATHLETES: CONDITIONING PROGRAMME

Aerobic and anaerobic age-related heart predictions (**R.H.R**) to (**M.H.R**), i.e. (**T.H.R**). Your workrate input is determined by your age relating to **maximum heart rate predictions** and training résumé. (**Refer to your R.H.R 65 b.p.m.**) (T.H.R. = Target Heart Rate).

Example: A **27 year old** athlete's work rate would be a maximum of **220 b.p.m.**—**27 years** equated with a pulse rate of **193 b.p.m. Hypothetical Resting Heart Rate (R.H.R) 65 b.p.m.**

Heart Rate Reserve (H.R.R.)

To exercise above this pulse rate, i.e. **193 b.p.m to 220 b.p.m.** could be dangerous! To determine your own age-related target heart-pulse rate, take your age (**in this example 27**) from **220 b.p.m. (193 b.p.m.)** to determine your **Target Heart Rate of 75-85%** of your **T.H.R.**

Your hypothetical pulse rate at rest (**R.H.R.**) = **65 b.p.m.** To determine your intensity of training:

(193-65 = 128 b.p.m) = (75% x 128) + (65 b.p.m.) = 161 b.p.m. =lower rate of intensity exercise. To improve **your aerobic capacity** and increase your anaerobic threshold, increase your exercise intensity to **(85% x 128b.p.m.) + 65 b.p.m (173-80) b.p.m**. Your target heart—rate **108.80 b.p.m** zone, **for at least 30 minutes of activity without rest**.

Repeated exercise résumé using your target heart-rate zone exercise intensity will produce a far greater and more efficient cardiovascular-respiratory functional capacity than any other activity.

Example: 27 year old = Lowest intensity—(161 b.p.m x 173.80 b.p.m). Highest M.H.R. predictions for 30 minutes' aerobic intensity exercises.

CARDIOVASCULAR ENDURANCE CAPACITY

To improve your endurance levels, you must cultivate your cardiovascularrespiratory functional capacity that is to create a greater (**VO2 max**) equates with (**The volume of oxygen uptake**) = (**per ml/kg/mm**) **of exercise**—to increase the levels of your aerobic and anaerobic threshold levels. Other ways to increase your endurance is to run a measured distance i.e. **1 mile** inside a stipulated time of **6 minutes or 2 miles x 12 minutes or 3 miles x 18 minutes**. Please convert to kilometres, do not run on hard surfaces.

THIS EXERCISEINTENSITY PREDICTION OF (58.20 V02 MAX), AN ACCEPTED LEVEL OF "CARDIOVASCULAR RESPIRATORY FUNCTIONAL CAPACITY".

PlyoDynamics + Power Kinetic Drills

These 'Plyo Dynamic WarmUp Drill's equate with 'Power Drill Workout's' which have been Field Tested by Professional's In the Field, such as Exercise Physiology,+ Branches of Physics plus 'Bio Mechanics of Human Movements' for Sports Participants, formulated by 'Professor of Exercise Physiology'. Dr Donald Chu PhD. www.donchu.com

'Scientific Fitness Analysis For All Sport'

Introducing **'Scientific Physiological Branches of Physics' ie; Human Movements relating to, 'Bio Mechanics + Kinesiology + Physiology'**, the three stages of a **'Professional Formula'** for **'Sport's Participation'**, require these **'Scientific Integrated Drills'**, entwining **'PlyoDynamic's** supplemented with **PlyoKinetics'** aerobically to develop **'High Power Drill's with Sport's Movement Pattern's of the Specific Sport** you are Participating In, as well as **'Endurance Aerobic Capacity Formula's'** so that you can move up to the next stage of your Training to develop a **'Scientific Program'** of **Plyo Metric's + PlyoKinetic's + PlyoDynamic's** to coordinate with these **'Three Stages of Progress'**.

The next development moves into **(Three Stages of, 1) 'Pre game WarmUp Drills'** which prepare your CardioVascular plus Respiratory System, in **'Specific Endurance Conditioning Programme'** laying the essential foundations to generate **'Sports Power Pack Drill's'** related to participate in **'Skill Specific Work-Outs'** mimicking specific movements and pattern's of play and ploy's and speed of execution during the actual **'Sports related Performance'** under tensed pressure situations in a **'Body Contact Sport'**.

"Leave your Brain behind, Leave the Game Behind"
(Stage 2),You are developing the secret of an exponential leap in **'Speed Endurance'** improving the **'Strength and Power of Skill Movement pattern's'** by optimising the functioning of your **'Nervous Impulse System'** promoting your **'Neuromuscular functioning Motor System'**, experiencing a leap in **'Automated Response Exercises'** to mimic the skills and movement patterns plus the intensities of your performance in the **'Sport of Your Choice'**, explosive implementation of your skills are formulated as you optimise your **'En gram System'** by mimicking the **'Skill Techniques'** of the **'Sport's Specific's'** and **'Automating Skill Responses'** in **'Pressure and Stress Situations'** in competitive Sport.

(Stage 3),**'The Six Modules'** you should target are to increase your **'Functional Work Capacity'** by increasing your ability to tolerate the ever increasing levels of **'Muscular Fatigue'**, brought on by the intensity of competition, your mission is to increase the **'Exercise Regime's'** that elevates your **A.R.T..H.E.R's Quest** for **'Elite Fitness**, by implementing and formulating **(Age Related Target Heart Exercise**

Six Modules for a Successful Conclusion in Sport

a), Planning and Preparation.

b), Injury Prevention Programme.

c), Mobility Skills and Drills.

d), Aerobic Endurance Grid's.

e). Speed and Agility Drill's.

f), Strength and Power grid's.

We envisage the implementation of our Futuristic Olympic 'Style Fitness Programme' will be the 'Pre Requisite Formula' for all Sport Participants to succeed.

PLODYNAMIC + POWERKINETIC DRILLS

Have been field tested by **'Senior Fitness Experts'** attached to our **S.R.E. Team** and is aimed specifically at Increasing your **Strength, Mobility, Agility + 'Aerobic Fitness'** functional capacities to an **'Elite Level of Application'**.

SCIENTIFIC FITNESS REVELATIONS

1. The Two Stages of Power Dynamics

These Scientific Drills help to **Develop Power** and specific movement pattern's of conditioning, as well as **Strength and Endurance** by promoting your **'Aerobic System'** to achieve your **"Age related Target Plateau"** as well as **'Pre Games Warm Up Exercises'**.

Power Conditioning used correctly, has a vital role in laying the foundations for generating your **Sports Specific Training Programme'**, mimicking both the movements and patterns and speed of the actual performance of the **'Technical Proficiency'** of the **'Sport of Your Choice'**, specific with the Technical movement patterns within the Boundaries of your Game.

By Implementing these **'Scientific Power and Conditioning Drills'**, your bodies **'Muscular System'** will be able to generate greater force efficiently dynamically and effectively to promote a optimisation of not only your **'Muscular System'** but also your **'Nervous System'**.

2. Your Power Workout specific to your Sport

These Power Exercise's improve your **Strength Power and Optimisation of Specific Movements** used in your **Sport**. You will achieve a leap in **Power and Stamina of Movements** by **Optimising the Muscular Function** facilitation of your **'Nervous + Motor Unit System'**.

To formulate activation of Relevant Skill's

To **Automate** under **Pressure Situations, Implement repetitive Drills** of the **Technical Proficient Skills** involved in the game, combined with grids of specific drills attaining to these Formulas, **Plyometric+ PlyoDynamic** + Power Endurance Exercises **Plyo-kinetic Drills**, using **Jump's, Hop's, Skip's, + Bounding, etc** that is applicable to **Power Drill's and Skill's** used in the **Sport of your Choice**.

'Plyo-Metrics' . . . 'Power-Kinetics' . . . 'Plyo-Dynamics'

Home Project 2008-2012 Diploma
15 Power-Dynamic Exercises

1. Standing Triple Jump

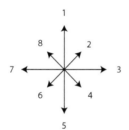

Equipment:

Cones. 8 Station Markers.

Start:

Stand with feet shoulder-width apart.

Action:

Push off both feet simultaneously and extend through the hips to land on one foot (hop), then push from this foot forward to land on the other foot (step), then jump from that foot extending the feet forward as far as possible.

2. Standing Triple Jump With Barrier Jump

Equipment:

A barrier.

Start:

Stand with feet shoulder-width apart.

Action:

Push off both feet simultaneously and extend through the hips to land on one foot (hop), then push from this foot forward to land on the other foot (step), then jump from that foot over the barrier, extending the feet forward as far as possible.

3. Pyramiding Box Hops

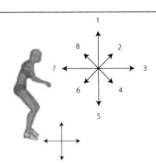

Equipment:

Three to five boxes of increasing height, evenly spaced 2 to 3 feet apart.

Start:

Distance In Between Each Station, 1 to 8 (30 m to 50 m) Count Number of Bound's + Skip's, Stand Jump's, Left Leg Hop's, Right Leg Hop's. Increase Number of Activity Over a Marked Distance (20m to 50m). Do not hold your Breath During Exercise Activity, Breathe Normally.

Action:

Jump onto the first box, then off on the other side, onto the second box, then off, and so on down the row.

4. Multiple Box-to-Box Squat Jumps

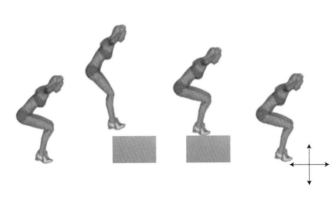

Equipment:

A row of boxes (all the same height, dependent on ability).

Action:

Jump to the first box, landing softly in a squat position. Maintaining the squat position, jump off the box on the other side and immediately onto and off of the following boxes. Keep hands on the hips or behind the head.

5. Multiple Box-to-Box Jumps With Single Leg Landing

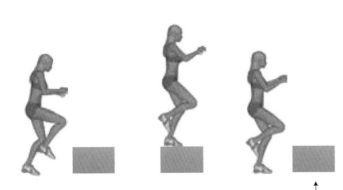

Equipment:

A row of boxes 6 to 12 inches high. (Later increase height to 18 to 24 inches.)

Action:

Jump onto the first box, landing on the takeoff foot, then jump to the floor, landing on the same foot. Continue in this fashion down the row of boxes. Repeat the exercise using the other leg.

Multiple Directional Activity After Each Station Exercise.
Alternate In Between Each Station.
Use (N.S.E.W. Directions), for Different Exercise.

6. Lateral Box Jump

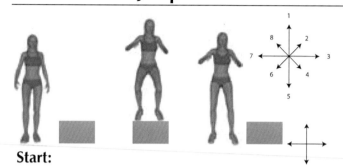

Action:

Jump onto the box and back to the ground on the other side. The exercise can he done as a single or as continuous movement across a line of 3 to 5 boxes of the same height (jumping to the ground between boxes).

Start:

Distance In Between Each Station, (30m to 50m) Count Number of Bound's + Skip's, Stand Jump's, Left Leg Hop's, Right Leg Hop's. Increase Number of Activity Over a Marked Distance (20m to 50m). Do not hold your Breath During Exercise Activity, Breathe Normally.

7. Front Box Jump

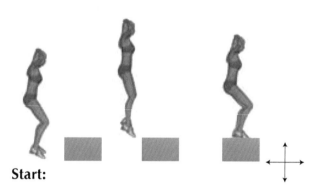

Action:

Jump up and land softly with both feet on the box. Step back down and repeat. For a more advanced exercise, hop down from the box and immediately jump back onto it. Use a variety of box heights, starting with 12 inch boxes, and building up to 42 inches with time.

Start:

Alternate Activities; Bounds, Hop's Skip's, Stand Jump's, 20 m Sprint's, Short Quick Stride + Medium Stride + Long Stride, With Knee's Up, Do not pump arm's Higher than Shoulder Level, Do not place Arms Across the Body when Executing any of the Sprint Exercises.

8. Squat Depth Jump

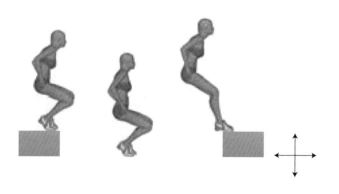

Action:

Step off the box and land in a 90degree squat position; explode up out of the squat and land solidly in a squat. For added difficulty, land on a second box of equal height after doing the jump.

9. Lateral Jump Over Barrier

Equipment:

One cone or hurdle.

Start:

Stand alongside the object to be cleared.

Action:

Jumping vertically but push sideways off the ground, bring the knees up to jump sideways over the barrier.

Multiple Directional Activity After Each Station Exercise.
Alternate In Between Each Station.
Use (N.S.E.W. Directions), for Different Exercise.

10. Standing Long Jump With Sprint

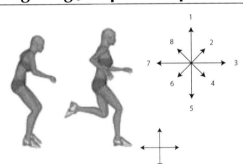

Equipment:

Start:

Stand in a semisquat with feet shoulderwidth apart.

Action:

Using a big arm swing, jump forward as far as possible. Upon landing sprint forward approximately 20 meters. Try to keep from collapsing on the landing land fully on both feet, then explode into a sprint.

11. Standing Long Jump With Change of Direction

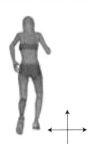

Equipment:

A grass field for safety.

Start:

Stand in a semisquat with feet shoulderwidth apart.

Action:

Using a big arm swing, jump forward as far as possible. Upon landing, immediately sprint to one of the 20 metre marks. Distance In Between Each Station, (30 m to 50 m) Count Number of Bound's + Skip's, Stand Jump's, Left Leg Hop's; Right Leg Hop's. Increase Number of Activity Over a Marked Distance (20m to 50m).

Multiple Directional Activity After Each Station Exercise. Alternate In Between Each Station.
Use (N.S.E.W. Directions), for Different Exercise.

12. Pyramid Box Hops

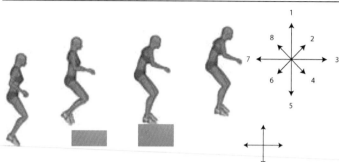

Action:

Jump onto the first box, then off on the other side, onto the second box, then off, and so on down the row.

13. Multiple Box-to-Box Jumps

Action:

Jump onto the first box, then off on the other side, onto the second box, then off, and so on down the row.

14. Multiple Box-to-Box Squat Jumps

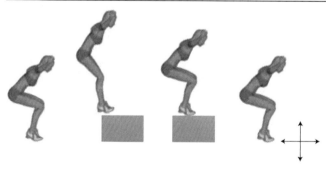

Action:

Jump onto the first box landing softly in a squat position. Maintaining the squat position, jump off the box on the other side and immediately onto and off the following boxes. Keep hands on the hips or behind the head.

15. Depth Jump With 180-Degree Turn

Action:

Step off the box and land on both feet. Immediately jump up and do a 180-degree turn in the air, landing again on both feet. For added difficulty, land on a second box after doing the turn.

Thesis 2007

Scientific Revelations Integrating Sports Science For A Successful Conclusion

Synopsis:

Simplified resume of these scientific formulations relevant to efficient **a) Sports Science Implementation, b) "Scientific Revelations"**, exploring Futuristic knowledge for elite sports propagation. **c) "Exercise Physiology "**, is related to a **Branch of Physics**, incorporating **Physiology + Bio Mechanics + Mechanical Kinesiology + Bio Kinetics**, integrating **(A, B, C,)** with **"Chemical Energy Formulation"**, through the **Aerobic Threshold**. The Aerobic System, is the exercise catalyst that promotes a chemical reaction. Mainly the production of **Mitochondria (See glossary) "Bio Chemically"**, through the **Cellular System**. These **Mitochondria** are the most important chemical formation of **ACh—Acetylcholine, :a chemical substance involved in important Physiological Functions such as transmission of an impulse connecting The Engram System (See glossary), via The C. N. S. Central Nervous System (See glossary): along the Electron Transport System (See glossary): via The Nodes of Ranvier, (forming the connection or junction of one neuron to another across a synaptic cleft)** facilitating impulses of the **Technical Proficiency**, of the related skill technique of the sport autonomically: **Under Stress + Pressure Situations**. To perform at an elite level and to achieve **A Successful Conclusion—The Aerobic System**: is the main activator to manufacture these magical **Mitochondria (See glossary)** in the cellular system. **LACK** of this **Sub cellular structure, decreases Acetyicholine Chemical Formulation, Elevating "Fatigue— Syndromes "**, not only **Physically**, but Second Degree symptoms of **Mental Fatigue**: as one would say **"Debilitating Progress"**. It seems the secret to a successful conclusion relies mainly within the **"Aerobic—System—Plateau—Levels"**, of age related target heart exercise rates to a maximum **(80% Capacity)**. This **(80%) Exercise Rate** stresses the Body's Functional Capacity, to cause a Bio Chemical Reaction + Formulation of these important **Mitochondria**, to promote an **"Injury Prevention Program"**, of exercise.

Chemical Energy Simplified + Aerobic System + Mitochondria

To be technical efficient plus physical proficient relies on the body's **Cellular System production** of **Chemical Energy** to diminish mental and physical **Fatigue Syndromes**. In the infrastructure of the Cellular System is the facilitation plus production of **(ATP)** in the **Chemical—Energy—System**, also known as **"The Krebs Cycle"**, (See glossary), which produces: **(ATP): Adenosine Triphosphate: (A complex chemical compound formed with the energy released from food and stored in cells: particularly muscles: only from energy released by the break down of this chemical compound can the cell perform its important work)**. Sub cellular vessels called **Mitochondria: (See glossary)**, are the manufacturers of a chemical transmitter called **(ACh) Acetylcholine (See glossary): involved in several important physiological functions relating to transmission of an impulse** i.e; Electronic Impulses from the **(C.N.S.) i.e; the Central Nervous System** + Electronic Transport System: called **Kinaesthetic receptors**, which perform body movements stored on **"Henry's Memory Drum"** : via the" **Engram System** ", (a memorised motor pattern stored in the brain; a permanent trace of technical proficiency skills implemented by a stimulus in the tissue protoplasm) **to produce when activated a specific sports participation skill.** This most important system does not function without **Aerobic Energy**: product of **The Krebs Cycle**.

Summary: This is the simplified knowledge of **Bio-Chemical Functions**, the coach or player is required to know. The catalyst for the **Continuous Activity without Fatigue**, is the chemical energy innovator,: the **Mitochondria**, without maximising **Mitochondria**, we reduce both the **"Mental and Physical Functioning Capacity"**.

Northern and Southern hemisphere Thesis

Bert & Margo Holcroft

Coaching Glossary

ACETYLCHOLLNE (ACh):—A chemical substance involved in several important physiological functions such as transmission of an impulse from one nerve fibre to another across a synapse.

ADENOSINE TRIPHOSPHATE (ATP):—A complex chemical compound formed with the energy released from food and stored in all cells, particularly muscles. Only from the energy released by the breakdown of this compound can the cell perform work.

ALL-OR-NONE LAW:—a stimulated muscle or nerve fibre contracts or propagates a nerve impulse either completely or not at all; in other words, a minimal stimulus causes a maximal response.

CENTRAL NERVOUS SYSTEM (C.N.S.):—The spinal cord and brain.

CONDITIONING:—Augmentation of the energy capacity of muscle through an exercise program. Conditioning is not primarily concerned with the skill of performance, as would be the case in training.

ENGRAM:—A memonsed motor pattern stored in the brain; a permanent trace left by a stimulus in the tissue protoplasm.

ELECTRON TRANSPORT SYSTEM (E.T.S.):—A series of chemical reactions occurring in **mitochondria**, in which electrons and hydrogen ions combine with oxygen to form water, and ATP is re synthesised. Also referred to as the :respiratory chain.

KREBS CYCLE:—A series of chemical reactions occurring in **mitochondria**, in which carbon dioxide is produced and hydrogen ions and electrons are removed from carbon atoms (oxidation). Also referred to as the tricarboxcylic acid cycle (T.C.A.), or citric acid cycle.

MAXIMAL OXYGEN COMSUMPTION (max V02):—The maximal rate at which oxygen can be consumed per minute; the power or capacity of the aerobic or oxygen system.

MITOCHONDRION (*singular*); **MITOCHONDRIA** (*plural*):—A sub cellular structure found in all aerobic cells in which the reactions of the Krebs Cycle and electron transport system take place.

MULTIPLE MOTOR UNIT SUMMATION:—The varying of the number of motor units contracting within a muscle at any given time.

MOTONEURON (MOTOR NEURON):—A nerve cell, which when stimulated, effects muscular contraction. Most motor neurons innervate skeletal muscle.

OXYGEN SYSTEM:—An aerobic energy system in which ATP is manufactured when food (principally sugar and fat) is broken down. This system produces ATP most abundantly and is the prime energy source during long lasting (endurance)

POSTSYNAPTIC NEURON:—A nerve cell located distal to a synapse.

RECEPTOR:—A sense organ that receives stimuli.

SPECIFICITY OF TRAINING:—Principle underlying construction of a training program for a specific activity or skill and the primary energy system(s) involved during performance.

TARGET HEART RATE (T.H.R.):—A pre determined heart rate to be obtained during exercise.

Rugby Accreditation

N.S.W. DEPARTMENT OF SPORT AND RECREATION

SPORTS ADMINISTRATION

This is to certify that

BERT HOLCROFT

has completed Level ...1...

SPORTS ADMINISTRATION COURSE FOR

Michael Cleary
Minister for Sport and Recreation
2/12/81 (Date)

THE RUGBY FOOTBALL LEAGUE
Senior Coaching Certificate

The undermentioned has attended a Rugby League Coaching Course and was examined by The Rugby Football League on (a) Laws of the Game and (b) Coaching Ability.

He has been awarded The Rugby Football League Senior Coaching Certificate.

Full Name H. Holcroft

Signed

1954

Secretary

Alec E. Fiddes Chief Coach

Holder's Signature H Holcroft

ACCREDITED III COACH BERT HOLCROFT

SPORTS ADMINISTRATION

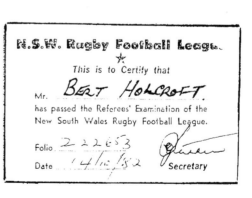

Coaching - Rugby - League, Rugby - Union.

THAT RUGBY SAGA OF FAMILY HOLCROFT

The Holcroft saga, a rugby story the like of which may never have been equalled in the history of the game. It begins over a century ago, when Mr. George Holcroft, was given charge of Leigh St. Peters R.L.F.C. in 1889.

He married and when his family grew up, Jack, Harry, William and Tom all played for local teams. They married and George's grandsons Bert and Bill also played.

Bert Holcroft has been a distinguished servant for the game of Rugby all his life. He holds coaching certificates from BOTH the Australian and British governing bodies—one of only a handful of men to achieve such an honour in the game's history.

For 20-odd years Bert Holcroft has had one of the unlikeliest jobs in sport—teaching Australian Rugby Coaches how to coach!

Considering the Australian dominance of World Rugby in recent years, that might seem a par with taking coal to Newcastle.

But make no mistake, Bert Holcroft has done as much as anyone to ensure Australia's re-emergence as a major Rugby power.

On the face of it, Australia wouldn't seem to need any outside help, let alone from a Pom. Their record of only one Test defeat since 1978 speaks for itself. But Bert's reputation is nation-wide "Down Under"—quite simply, he's one of the best in the business.

Bert, who played for Leigh between 1950-60, has spent much of his latter years Down Under lecturing to top-grade coaches in New South Wales.

Born and bred in Cameron Street, Leigh, Bert has few peers when it comes to teaching the basics of the 13-a-side game. Since emigrating in the late 60's, Bert has dedicated his life to coaching and fitness techniques. Teams in Queensland, New South Wales and Sydney have all come under his influence—often with spectacular results. Bert's credentials are impeccable.

Last summer, he achieved the highest accolade in Australia—his Grade Three Certificate personally signed by the then Australian league chairman Kevin Humphreys and the Director of Coaching, Peter Corcoran. Three years earlier, Bert sailed through his Grades One and Two with flying colours. In 1953, he was awarded his Senior Coaching Certificate in England.

Bert, who held a number of posts at Hilton Park before emigrating to Australia, has spent a lot of his time heavily involved with Rugby in the universities there. He became director of coaching for the University of New South Wales and later coach of the Combined Universities side.

Coaching Accreditation awarded by the Australian Institute of Sport, Department of Sport and Recreation NSW and the NSW Rugby League for administration, as well as being awarded National Coaching Certificates in both Britain and Australia—one of only a handful of people to do so.

Eventually, the offer of a job in Sydney came—to coach Premiership glamorous club, Eastern Suburbs.

World Accredited Coaching Seminar
SPORTS MANUALS

2013 UPGRADES

Bert Holcroft
Author
& Course Director

Margo Holcroft
Author
& Course Director

Foreword of contents by
Sir Clive Woodward OBE
Associate 2002-2009
Former England RU
Director of Rugby
World Cup 2003 Winner
London Olympics 2012
Elite Performance Director

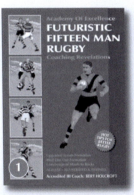

1. Academy Of Excellence — **FUTURISTIC FIFTEEN MAN RUGBY** — Coaching Revelations — Accredited III Coach: BERT HOLCROFT

2. BOOK TWO — **FUTURISTIC RUGBY LEAGUE** — ADVANCED FUTURISTIC "THIRTEEN MAN RUGBY" — AGELESS – ILLUSTRATED & DEFINED — Accredited III Coach: BERT HOLCROFT

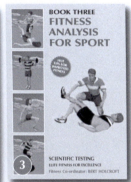

3. BOOK THREE — **FITNESS ANALYSIS FOR SPORT** — SCIENTIFIC TESTING — ELITE FITNESS FOR EXCELLENCE — Fitness Co-ordinator: BERT HOLCROFT

4. BOOK FOUR — **SOCCER REVELATIONS COACHING KNOWLEDGE** — FITNESS AND TRAINING REGIMES — PEAK FITNESS AND SOMATOGRAPH CHARTS — Accredited III Coach: BERT HOLCROFT

5. Learn@Home Project — Academy of Excellence eBook No. 5 — **Fifteen Man Rugby** — Rugby Union — Personal Skills & Fitness Drills — FREE — www.sportsrevent.com

6. Learn@Home Project — Academy of Excellence eBook No. 6 — **Thirteen Man Rugby** — Rugby League — Personal Skills & Fitness Drills — FREE — www.sportsrevent.com

Plyometric Fitness Drills by
Dr Donald Chu PhD
Associate 1980-2010
USA Olympic
Participants Consultant
www.donchu.com

Foreword of contents by
Jimmy Smith
FA Coach
Ex Burnley FC, Ex Fulham FC
Ex Leyton Orient FC
Associate

www.sportsrevent.com

Sports Revelation Enterprises
Open Book Coaching @ Home Project 2010-2012 Diploma

Upgraded revelations Sports Courses / Manuals featuring a Full Administration Section -
Upgraded Technical Proficiencies - Fitness & Fully Formulated Coaching Course

Printed in the United States
By Bookmasters